Daughters of Imani: A Christian Rites of Passage for African-American Young Women

Planning Guide

Richelle B. White

Abingdon Press
Nashville

Copyright © 2005 by Abingdon Press. All rights reserved.

With the exception of those items so noted, no part of this work may be reproduced or transmitted in any form or by any means, electronic or mechanical, including photocopying and recording, or by any information storage or retrieval system, except as may be expressly permitted by the 1976 Copyright Act or in writing from the publisher. Requests for permission should be addressed to Abingdon Press, 201 Eighth Avenue, South, P.O. Box 801, Nashville, TN 37202-0801.

Scripture quotations, unless otherwise indicated, are from the *New Revised Standard Version of the Bible*, copyright © 1989, Division of Christian Education of the National Council of the Churches of Christ in the United States of America. Used by permission. All rights reserved.

MANUFACTURED IN THE UNITED STATES OF AMERICA

Richelle B. White is an ordained Baptist minister and the pastor of the Zion Baptist Church in King and Queen, Virginia. Rev. White is a graduate student at Union Theological Seminary and Presbyterian School of Christian Education, in Richmond. From 1993 to 2000, she established and facilitated a rites of passage program for African-American girls at Payne Chapel African Methodist Episcopal Church, in Baltimore, Maryland. The program continued for three additional years after she left to pursue further graduate studies. Rev. White has traveled nationally and internationally, spreading the Word of God through the ministry of Christian Education.

05 06 07 08 09 10 11 12 13 14—10 9 8 7 6 5 4 3 2 1

Contents

From the Author: Rev. Richelle B. White 4
A Theologian's Point of View: Bishop Vashti McKenzie 6
A Psychologist's Point of View: Dr. Sheila Peters 7

PART 1: THE PROGRAM 8
Chapter 1: A Christian Rites of Passage for African-American Young Women 9
Chapter 2: Organizational Structure 13
Chapter 3: Designing Your Program 16
Chapter 4: Mentors' Training 20
Chapter 5: Membership 35
Chapter 6: Other Components 38
Chapter 7: Rituals and Ceremonies 41

PART 2: THE CURRICULUM 56
Curriculum Overview 58

Unit 1: Self-Worth and Self-Esteem 60
1. Self-Image and the Media (Hip-Hop Culture) 61
2. Declaration of Self-Esteem 64
3. Developing Healthy Self-Esteem 70
4. Relationships With Christ and Others 74

Unit 2: Endurance and Bonding/Family Matters 77
1. My Family, Me, and You 78
2. Understanding My Family 81
3. Praying for One Another 83
4. Heritage 86

Unit 3: Health and Sexuality 93
1. Self-Image and the Media 94
2. Responsible Sexuality and Celibacy 98
3. Sexually Transmitted Diseases and HIV/AIDS 102
4. HIV/AIDS: 'The Truth Shall Set You Free' 107

Unit 4: Social Grace 111
1. Character in Social Life and Relationships 112
2. Table Hospitality 114
3. Beauty and Bounty 117
4. Time and Money Management 121

Emerging Womanhood Graduate Exam 126
Resources Page 127
Bibliography 128

From the Author

Something on the Inside, Working on the Outside

(An African-American Congregational Song)

Something on the inside,

Working on the outside.

Oh, what a change in my life!

I've got something on the inside,

And it's working on the outside.

Oh, what a change in my life!

I've got something on the inside,

And it's working on the outside.

Oh, what a change in my life!

I've got Jesus on the inside,

And he's working on the outside.

Oh, what a change in my life! (*3 times*)

I've got the Holy Ghost on the inside,

And he's working on the outside.

Oh, what a change in my life! (*3 times*)

This congregational song (at left), which is often sung during praise and worship services in African-American churches, speaks of an outward manifestation that can take place in a person's life as a result of an inward transformation. As a youth empowerment cultivator, it is my belief that every child, regardless of race, color, or economic status, is searching for a deeper meaning in life. Youth seek to fill the chasm that plagues their everyday existence. Too often, they seek to fill it through sex, violence, alcohol, drugs, and conformity. As they continue to search for the deeper meaning in life, many of them are being deceived and are falling prey to devices that seek to steal, kill, and destroy God's purpose for their lives.

God is speaking us today, just as in the days of the Bible, charging us to "Train children in the right way, and when old, they will not stray" (Proverbs 22:6). In John 14:6, Jesus says, "I am the way, and the truth, and the life. No one comes to the Father except through me." Thus we have a charge to keep, a charge to bring our youth to holistic adulthood by introducing them to the triune God, who is able to transform all life. In response to this charge, for nine years beginning in 1994, the Sisters in the Spirit (SIS) Rites of Passage and Mentoring Ministry sought to give young women and girls the opportunity to meet and experience God at their level of need and help them discover the purpose and plan that God has for their life.

In the 1980s, a strategic movement was made in the African-American community to create Afro-centric rites of passage programs for African American boys. Dr. Jawanza Kunjufu brought a much-needed perspective concerning the plight of African-American boys, within the realm of public education. His three-volume work, *Countering the Conspiracy to Destroy Black Boys*, is a critical blue print that explains the need for the African-American community to join together to do something to solve the problem. As a result, African-American communities throughout the United States developed programs that would help lead African-American boys to successful manhood. All of this emphasis on the African-American male child ignited a flame within, causing me to pose the question, "What about the African-American female child?" She suffers as well in ways particular to gender.

Before I was aware of what was happening, my passion for this population grew; I started to search for literature about faith-based rites of passage programs for the African-American girl. Much to my surprise, I could not find any literature of that specific nature. I found a wealth of information about Afro-centric rites but none about faith-based rites for females. This shortage compelled me to launch out into the deep to create a faith-based rites of passage model.

Initially, SIS (now Daughters of Imani) was an idea that developed into a graduate research study. This study developed into an interdenominational rites of passage and mentoring ministry for females ages 8–18. The program operated for nine years at Payne Memorial African Methodist Episcopal Church, in Baltimore, Maryland. My pastor, Rev. Dr. Vashti M. McKenzie, now Bishop McKenzie, was a constant source of support and encouragement. The women of Payne Memorial and women of other churches throughout the Baltimore Metropolitan area served faithfully and diligently as agents of change to the next generation of African-American females. God's Spirit was poured out on this ministry. It grew from twenty participants to more than one hundred. SIS received recognition from city and state officials in Baltimore and the state of Maryland, the Maryland State Mentoring Resource Center, the National Mentoring Partnership, *Newsweek Magazine*, and Kaplan Educational Services.

God has given a command and a vision so that the youth will not perish due to a lack of knowledge. Prayerfully, you too will catch the vision and use your unique gifts and talents to empower the next generation of girls as they make the journey to holistic Christian womanhood. We pray that the information in this book will inspire you to join us in making a difference. As I seek to join the ranks of those who have provided and continue to provide sound scholarship and models for replication, I wish to acknowledge Mary C. Lewis, Mafori Moore, Bernida Thompson, Nsenga Warfield-Coppock, and Madeline Wright—predecessors in the rites of passage ministry. This book is dedicated to Patricia A. White Carroll, my mother and encourager; Bishop Vashti McKenzie, a Visionary Trailblazer; Sisters in the Spirit mentors and participants; and my sisters in Christ and the ministry. I appreciate their steadfastness, commitment, and diligence in working on behalf of those who are most vulnerable—African-American girls. I pray that others will join the crusade by using the *Daughters of Imani: A Christian Rites of Passage for African American Young Women* curriculum as they heed the call to "train up a child."

A Theologian's Point of View

By Bishop Vashti Murphy McKenzie

The term *rites of passage* is not foreign to the African-American community. From ancient Egyptian society to modern-day Black America, the "rite" has been the fundamental method of ensuring continuity of culture for Africans across the Diaspora.

Generations of Black people throughout the Diaspora have prepared adolescents to cross over the threshold of adulthood. Today, this tradition continues in an effort to ensure that the basic values of our culture and heritage are passed from one generation to the next.

To perpetuate this tradition, Richelle has created *Sisters in the Spirit—A Faith-Based Rites of Passage Manual for the Adolescent and Preadolescent Female.** This work skillfully bridges the gap between community and faith-based "rites" programs by presenting a curriculum that is culturally relevant yet that allows us to pass on the heritage of the Christian faith.

The Sisters in the Spirit model initially began as a graduate research study by the author and, after years of hard work and commitment, stands as a model for replication by other faith and community-based organizations.

Richelle introduces a work that is both theological and practical. She presents the history of the rites of passage movement with accuracy and clarity. Her research is thorough and complete. The program design allows for efficient implementation. The curriculum is engaging and relevant to the "Hip-Hop" culture. Thus, before you is a work that has the power to transform the lives of today's youth.

However, this work is more than a manual to be used with adolescent and preadolescent girls. It is the testament of the author's struggle with her own faith journey, and her determination to find and fulfill God's plan and purpose for her life. In finding her God-given purpose, Richelle has found a niche in reaching, teaching, and discipling the next generation for Christ.

I commend this work to you and pray that you will "catch the vision" and join us in the tradition of transmitting our rich spiritual and cultural heritage to the next generation.

—**Bishop Vashti Murphy McKenzie**
  Presiding Prelate, Thirteenth Episcopal District
  African Methodist Episcopal Church

* Now known as *Daughters of Imani: A Christian Rites of Passage for African-American Young Women*

A Psychologist's Point of View

By Dr. Sheila Peters*

Womanhood is a special gift that girls and women must grow to appreciate. Rites of passage models provide a training ground for generations of females to share and confront the challenges and delights of being female. *Daughters of Imani: A Christian Rites of Passage for African-American Young Women* is a curriculum that provides a framework for adult women with a Christian foundation to embrace the challenge of navigating young females through the developmental pathway to womanhood. Through the modeling of essential attributes of positive womanhood, the users of this curriculum can provide a supportive environment designed to enrich the lives of girls. Girls will learn how to confront their strengths and challenges and seek a pathway to positive personal development.

The social, emotional, intellectual, psychological, and spiritual needs of girls must be supported through opportunities for self-growth and personal development. Positive relationships through mentoring activities can prepare girls for a journey into positive womanhood. Girls give attention to interpersonal relationships and are confronted with the importance of how others see them. During puberty, girls may be subjected to the scrutiny of others who seek to control the girls' interactions. Emphasis on her physical development overshadows her emotional, psychological, and spiritual development. Although her physical development is central to their overall health, girls need nurturing relationships, from women in particular, as they journey to womanhood.

In addition to providing the framework for a positive learning environment, *Daughters of Imani* is rooted in the cultural heritage of African-American girls. With a clear understanding of cultural strengths and the legacy of many ancestors who have contributed under harsh circumstances, an African-American girl can be introduced to strong African-American heroines. She may be able to see herself as having the possibility of contributing to her world. Cultural pride and an appreciation for others are significant factors in positive ethnic identity development.

Self-esteem is particularly vulnerable during the transition from childhood to adolescence. The need for acceptance within peer groups in the communities and schools may shape decision-making during this transitional phase. Modern society contributes to the shift of the importance of the peer group. Overworked, underpaid parents may work in inflexible employment settings that make it difficult for parents to support their children. Financial constraints can restrict basic parental involvement in children's schools and monitoring of children's behavior. Many young people are growing up in single-parent, female-headed households, some of whom are able to function as both mother and father. However, parents, whether single or married can be distracted and/or overwhelmed by their economic and social responsibilities, with little energy or understanding to nurture the delicate esteem and self-image of their daughters.

Gender and ethnic identity development are crucial tasks for African-American children as they transition through adolescence, regardless of the family or economic structure. Upper middle-class African-American girls are likely to be in minority status in their social/educational environments, where Caucasian images of beauty are reinforced. As these girls attempt to associate with their cultural heritage, they may be faced with mainstream social systems that minimize the importance of cultural heritage. African-American girls need African-American women to teach, instruct, nurture, and support them in their transition through adolescence to young adulthood. Participation in a rites of passage program can provide young women with additional adult support and an alternative peer group by which positive self-esteem can more readily flourish.

Daughters of Imani is biblically and spiritually based. The biblical foundation offers a perspective that will help define positive womanhood for girls. With a spiritual foundation, young girls who are transitioning through puberty can become equipped with the personal, emotional, and social fabric to combat sexualized media images and negative peer pressure. Moreover, this curriculum provides the structure by which women in church and community groups can more easily develop the mentoring opportunities in which girls can discover their abilities, their personal strengths, and their creativity. With a rites of passage rooted in a spiritual framework, girls may be able to enhance their spiritual development as they search for meaning in the complexity of life.

* Dr. Sheila Peters is a Nashville-based psychologist who specializes in working with adolescent African-American girls. She also teaches at Fisk University.

PART 1:
The Program

Chapter 1

A Christian Rites of Passage for African-American Young Women

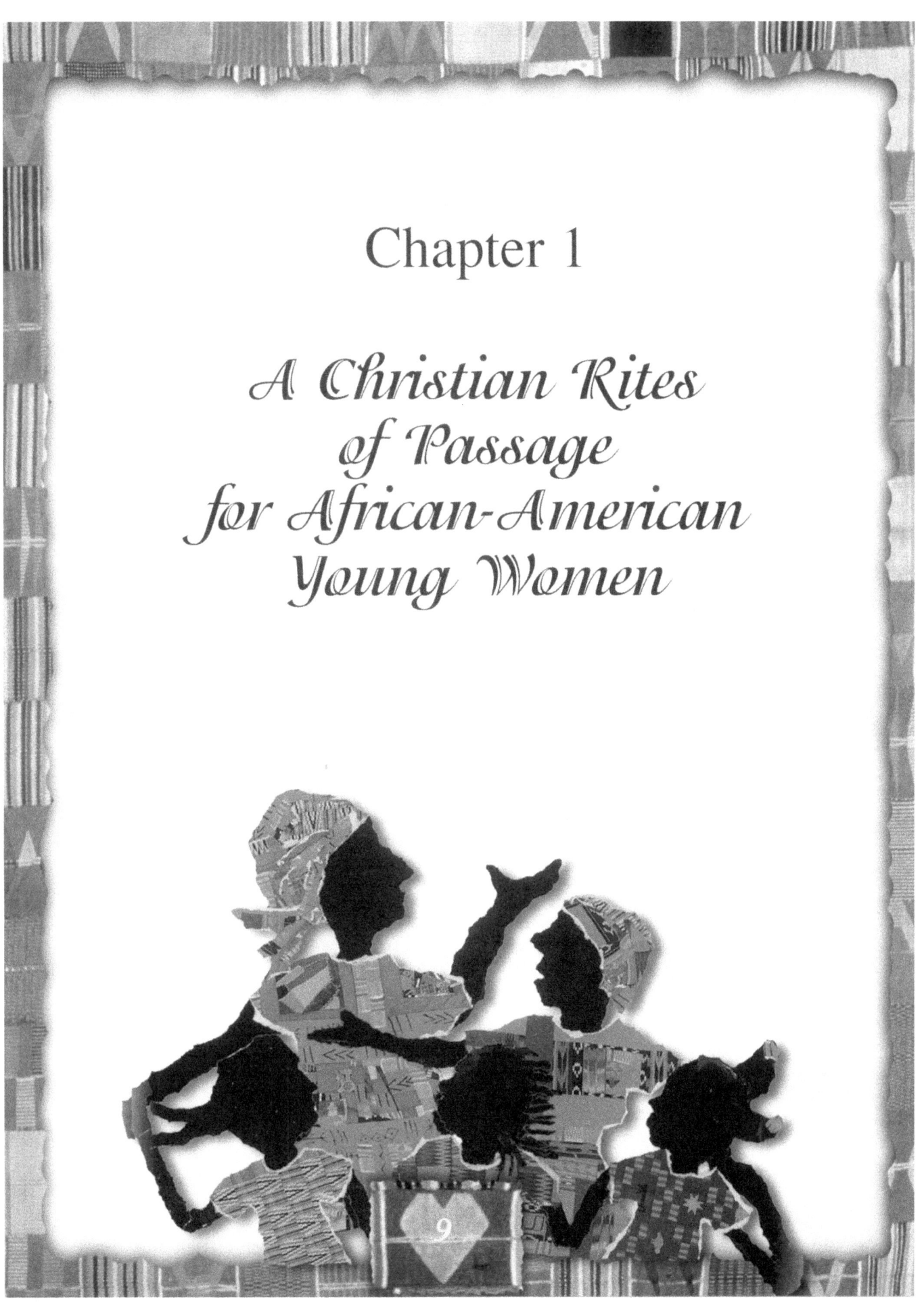

From 1994 to 2003, the Payne Memorial African Methodist Episcopal Church, in Baltimore, Maryland, was the home of Sisters in the Spirit—A Journey Toward Womanhood Rites of Passage and Mentoring Ministry. In its nine years of existence, this ministry provided a comprehensive (physical, emotional, intellectual, social, and spiritual) curriculum, plus one-to-one and group mentoring experiences for the participants. The program emphasized Christian and African values, and the adult mentors were drawn from the church membership and parents of the participants. Abingdon Press is pleased to offer the Sisters in the Spirit program as part of a publication entitled *Daughters of Imani: Christian Rites of Passage for African-American Young Women*. This resource includes a planning guide with curriculum areas, a Bible study curriculum (*Daughters of Imani: Young Women's Bible Study*), and a Black history component (*Daughters of Imani Celebration of Women.*) Daughters of Imani is a Christian rites of passage and mentoring program. It supplies specific programmatic guidelines for working with young African-American women ages 8–18. It is the sister program to *Young Lions: Christian Rites of Passage for African-American Young Men*, by Chris McNair.

STATEMENT OF VISION
Proverbs 29:18 (KJV) states very simply: "Where there is no vision the people perish." While mentoring programs are a good idea to help young ladies become responsible members of society, programs without a clearly articulated vision will be without direction. Vision provides direction that must be communicated to all participants. Both youth and adults desire to be a part of a ministry that has a clear reason for its existence. They will follow if they know where they are going and they agree with the destination. People are attracted to ministries that honor their time and provide meaning for their lives. People highly value their time, and are reluctant to become involved if they sense a lack of direction.

In Africa, women uphold the society's traditions and encourage community and fellowship. These women nurture younger women, teaching and molding them into responsible, mature, faithful women. Women reach out to younger women, regardless of familial or actual kinship relationships. Older women are considered mothers, younger women are daughters, and women of comparable age are sisters. All are united as daughters of God.

Daughters of Imani offers a structured Christian ministry by which to reclaim that which was lost in the transition from Africa to America. Because God commands that ministry have vision, the Daughters of Imani statement of vision is:

To educate and empower African-American young women ages 8–18 to become Christian leaders in the twenty-first century.

STATEMENT OF MISSION
Just as important as vision, is a sense of mission. Mission is the methodology used to achieve the vision of an organization or ministry. The methodology for Daughters of Imani is a rites of passage program, a structure by which permission is granted by a community to move to a higher level of social status in the process of human development. "Rites" are specific activities that participants must successfully complete. "Passage" signifies the movement from one level to the next. All of the girls and women are referred to as "Daughters of Imani." The girls in the program are designated as initiates. The women of the program plan the rites (program activities) and mentor the girls through the completion of the program.

Rites assist the young women in developing self-esteem, knowledge, and social skills. These rites also enable the young women to begin planning for the future in terms of vocational or college education, career aspirations, and financial planning. Through the process, a deepening knowledge of biblical women and their stories, the presence of God in their lives, and the indwelling power of the Holy Spirit as motivator and strengthener are emphasized. Young women will discover their gifts, talents, intellect, and creativity along with integrity and a striving to make a difference in their communities and world. The mission statement articulates the methodology by which the program will achieve its vision: To provide a comprehensive (physical, emotional, intellectual, social, and spiritual) Bible-based curriculum, plus one-to-one and group mentoring experiences for adolescent and preadolescent females to help them chart their course to holistic womanhood.

STATEMENT OF PURPOSE
Equally as important as vision and mission is purpose. Purpose defines the reason for the existence of something. The purpose of the Daughters of Imani

program is to develop Christian leaders for the twenty-first century by providing an ongoing program of character education, leadership development, and meaningful mentoring relationships for young women between the ages of eight and eighteen—that is, the period of adolescence. Adolescence can be likened to the concept of a desert. The desert is a place of extremes, and so is adolescence. If our young women are to survive and thrive during this critical developmental stage, it is crucial that they have life-sustaining support systems to help through this tumultuous time. The Daughters of Imani program can provide such a support system. This program educates the participants through prepared teachings, exercises, and experiences that will lead them through a safe, successful, and fulfilling passage into adulthood.

THEOLOGY

Daughters of Imani is a Christian rites of passage program. The word *Imani* (ee-MAH-nee) is Swahili for "faith." The program is built on a theology that affirms the love and grace of Jesus Christ. The activities are designed to help participants deepen their faith in God through Jesus Christ. All participants of the program are encouraged to give their lives to Jesus Christ, join a church, and become more active in their Christian journey. The activities may ease a transformative experience, enabling all Daughters of Imani to become witnesses for the power of God in their families and community.

Participants are also encouraged to deepen their faith in one another as women. From Leah and Rachel (Genesis 30), to Hannah and Peninnah (1 Samuel 1), to Mary and Martha (Luke 10:38-42), women have often seen one another as competitors. Program participants should model the relationship of Naomi and Ruth or Elizabeth and Mary, developing strong bonds of love and trust for one another. Daughters of Imani must strive to look at one another with the unconditional love of Christ.

Jesus teaches that we should love our neighbors as ourselves. All Daughters of Imani are encouraged to deepen faith in self. The program promotes self-love. All Daughters of Imani are encouraged to love themselves, to love everything about themselves, from their physical appearance, to their personality characteristics, to those aspects of themselves that are evolving for the better. Daughters of Imani are called to experience the indwelling love of God and the radiating love of the family around them in order to increase their feelings of self-love, and then to express that love back in relationships with the family and in love of God.

"And the child grew and became strong in spirit" (Luke 1:80). The Sisters in the Spirit program upon which this resource is based used the word *spirit* as an acronym (see page 12).

Young women who participate in this program have a unique opportunity to grow strong in spirit, in the knowledge of God and self. The experience in sisterhood can provide a foundation that will help participants live out the vision, mission, purpose, and theology of *Daughters of Imani: Christian Rites of Passage for African-American Young Women.*

Self-Discipline

Purpose

Integrity

Respect

Ingenuity

Time Management

Chapter 2

Organizational Structure

A Daughters of Imani program is organized by a "Council of Women Elders." These are women who come together and covenant to work and share on behalf of African-American women, young and old. The Council may start with two women with a vision but, with prayer and planning, will grow to include all of those who will provide or select leadership for the program, including the administrative team, mentors, circle leaders, instructors, and so forth. The director, called *Ohemma* (oh-HEH-mah), heads the council. The word *Ohemma* means "female ruler." In the Akan culture of Ghana and the Ivory Coast, the Ohemma is traditionally the queen mother of a local tribe. She is the co-ruler of the tribe and shares with the king responsibility over political and administrative affairs. The royal court selects the Ohemma. In Daughters of Imani, the Council of Women will select the Ohemma, who serves as the director of the entire program.

The responsibilities of the Ohemma include contacting women to join the Council of Women, delegating jobs and projects to members of the council, planning and organizing team meetings and mentor training, and reaching out to women who can be circle leaders. She, along with the administrative team, is responsible for making sure that mentors and circle leaders receive appropriate training.

ADMINISTRATIVE TEAM

The administrative team includes the Ohemma/Director, the Assistant Director, Public Relations Chair, Treasurer, Fundraising Chair, and the Sisters of Niara (nee-YAH-rah) Coordinator.

Ohemma/Director
Δ Prepares the agenda for administrative team meetings
Δ Leads the meetings and make assignments
Δ Inspires other leaders
Δ Organizes the Journey Toward Womanhood Conference
Δ Provides direction for curriculum and instructional choices
Δ Provides for Bible study leaders

Assistant Director
Δ Performs the duties of the Director whenever needed
Δ Directs the planning and execution of special events
Δ Reserves meeting space, requisitions checks, and distributes them
Δ Provides orientation for new mentors
Δ Orders supplies and materials
Δ Encourages and assists the membership

Administrative Assistant
Δ Takes the minutes of the administrative team meetings
Δ Maintains attendance records

Public Relations Chair
Δ Writes, compiles, and distributes a newsletter
Δ Reminds the administrative team of monthly meetings
Δ Maintains a written and pictorial record of the activities of the organization

Treasurer
Δ Maintains records of expenses
Δ Develops the budget with the assistance of the administrative team

Fundraising Chair
Δ Directs the fundraising

Sisters of Niara Coordinator
Δ Develops and facilitates the teen leadership component (Imani/Niara School of Servant Leadership)
Δ Plans the monthly Sisters of Niara meetings
Δ Schedules community service projects
Δ Assists with planning of retreats and conferences

CIRCLE LEADERS

Circle leaders are the link between the administrative team, the participants, and the parents. They are the elders who carry out the group-mentoring component in the small study groups–the Sister Circles. These women have a heart to work with female adolescents. They are devoted to carrying out the actual functioning of the program with participants in forming relationships and implementing activities. Circle leaders are responsible for teaching/facilitating the curriculum. Circle leaders and group participants plan and execute a community outreach project during the program year. The Sister Circles can be divided according to age and/or grade, depending on your community. Circles meet no fewer than twice each month for study and fellowship.

A circle leader does the following:
Δ Prepares small group learning experiences
Δ Handles refreshments for the group
Δ Secures supplies and materials as necessary
Δ Keeps participants' attendance records
Δ Communicates with the pubic relations chair, concerning newsletter items
Δ Follows up with participants concerning activities and attendance

INSTRUCTORS (optional)
An instructor does the following:
Δ Teaches a lesson on one of the designated areas of study chosen by the council

ONE-TO-ONE MENTORS
A mentor does the following:
Δ Makes a commitment to spend a minimum of 52 hours a year (if possible) with at least one assigned participant.
Δ Works with more than one participant if availability allows (Individual time is the goal.)

SPECIAL EVENTS COORDINATORS
A special event coordinator does the following:
Δ Is responsible for field trips and special events
Δ Prepares time and place logistical details according to schedule
Δ Communicates budgeting needs, according to schedule
Δ Orders supplies and materials, according to budget approval
Δ Solicits volunteers and chaperones to assist in carrying out the functions

HELPERS
These are women who are not able to serve as elders or mentors but agree to assist the program in whatever way they can: chaperoning field trips, making decorations, providing materials, providing food, giving talks, providing music, and so forth.

PARENTS/FAMILY ELDER
Parental/Family Elder involvement and support is crucial to the success of the Daughters of Imani program. They are in partnership with the Council of Women in helping participants journey through the program. One of the strengths of the African-American family is the flexibility of its definition and configuration. A Daughters of Imani program should be as inclusive as possible in terms of who is a parental figure. However, persons fulfilling the role of parents are required to attend the Fall Open House in order to become better acquainted with the program. While they do not have to hold church membership, they are asked to accept the Christ-centered theological foundations of Daughters of Imani. Parents must agree to show accountability to the program by transporting their children to and from ministry activities and/or by providing some other kind of assistance that may be needful.

Parents are encouraged to assist their daughters in maintaining the requirements for Daughters of Imani participants. They are expected to communicate with and lend their support to the leadership. Parents should be knowledgeable of program activities by reading the newsletter and communicating with their daughters. They are expected to assist the program however they can: accompanying field trips, making decorations, providing materials, food, giving talks, providing music, participating in ministry fundraisers, making monetary donations.

PARTICIPANTS
All girls are expected to accept the discipline, structure, and Christian foundation of the program. All must be at least eight years old or in the third grade. They must attend the Fall Open House and faithfully adhere to the code of conduct and membership requirements. Participants are encouraged to take advantage of leadership opportunities.

Participants are required to practice reciprocity in the mentoring relationship by being considerate in advising mentors and circle leaders of necessary absences. The girls must work with their mentors and parents to meet fundraising requirements. They must complete their program portfolios and projects on schedule.

Chapter 3

Planning for Daughters of Imani

The Daughters of Imani program offers a simple process, easily adaptable by any organization or group that works with young women. This model has been specifically designed to be a faith-based rites of passage and mentoring ministry for African-American young women. However, it can be modified for use by school and community groups, as well as different ethnic groups. The key to success is commitment and flexibility. There are countless ways to design a program that meets the needs of your particular group. Starting a Daughters of Imani program at your church or community center is as easy as contacting women who have an interest in girls and young women, as well as their spiritual and formative development.

MAKE CONTACT

Begin with friends, associates, family ties, and women's groups. Call and visit area churches, sororities, Links groups, and other organizations. Make plans to address meetings of organizations, talk with individual women, and so forth.

BRING WOMEN TOGETHER

Invite several women to come together in an informal setting to discuss developmental issues facing African-American young girls. Don't start by asking the women to make a commitment or to begin a program. Bring them together just to talk. Have refreshments, prayer; play light music. Make it a social yet spiritual atmosphere. The goal is for women to bond, to make connections, and to enjoy one another's company. As the group engages in discussion and reflection, they will naturally begin to talk about their personal lives and experiences with family, faith, womanhood, race, and other issues. This time together will allow you to affirm common ideals so that the group may be of one accord.

SHARE THE VISION

Have a second meeting or informal gathering. You are now in the process of developing a Council of Women/Elders. At this meeting, be more specific about asking individuals to participate in the Daughters of Imani program. At this point, many will have begun to invest personally in the vision of mentoring girls to help them become women. It is not the number of women gathered that is critical to the success of the program but their commitment. A program of high quality will attract women of high quality. Describe the different functions and roles. Ask the women to think about what role they envision themselves playing.

As the Council of Women considers designing and implementing a faith-based rites of passage program for the community, the first task is to identify the motivations for doing so. In a Christ-centered program, everything should be done by prayer and petition and with thanksgiving, presenting concerns and requests to God (Philippians 4:6). Before undertaking any type of ministry with young people, the counsel of God should be sought. Use these Scriptures and questions for individual and corporate meditation in discerning the motivations for developing a Daughters of Imani program:

Colossians 3:23-25

Δ What are my reasons for wanting to create a rites of passage program?
Δ Am I seeking to become a hero and receive recognition for undertaking this task?

Romans 12:1-2

Δ Am I willing to present my body to Christ for the work of the ministry?
Δ Am I willing to be transformed by the Word of God, that God's will may be accomplished through me?
Δ Being transformed may include giving up some behaviors that may not be pleasing to God. What are some of those behaviors?
Δ Will any of these behaviors hinder my effectiveness with young people?

Galatians 5:22-23

Δ What are the personality characteristics that God requires Christians to have?
Δ With which of these characteristics am I struggling to exhibit in my daily life?
Δ Which of these characteristics does God need to develop in my life?

Psalm 37:5

Δ What do I need to commit unto the Lord?
Δ What do I want the Lord to bring to pass in my life?

Matthew 7:7-8

Δ As I consider being part of developing a rites of passage ministry, for what am I asking God?
Δ What am I seeking for?
Δ What doors am I praying to be opened?

Matthew 18:19-20
Δ With what other leadership has God called me to work? What are their names?
Δ Are we in agreement with one another?
Δ About what are we in agreement?
Δ What are our collective prayer requests?

A rites of passage program of any kind is a program that will put the needs of young people first. In working with young women, a person must be sure in the knowledge of who she is and why she wants to work with this population. Continue in a meditative process by asking these questions:

Δ Why do I want to work with the African-American female?
Δ What skills do I possess that would assist me in the development of this program?
Δ What are my talents?
Δ What do I know about today's female youth culture?
Δ What do I like and dislike about today's youth culture?
Δ Is it my objective to change the girls and dissuade them from being active participants in their culture?
Δ Am I willing to learn more about today's youth culture so that I may be effective in working with them?
Δ What are my spiritual gifts?
Δ How can I make a difference?

Other questions may arise that those designing the program may wish to explore. Allow for a period of evaluation, and analyze of conclusions. When the Council has determined that its motivations are in line with God's will and purpose for a rites of passage ministry, it is time to proceed.

DEVELOPING A STATEMENT OF PURPOSE
The next step is to move forward with the development of a statement of purpose. A purpose statement will clarify the God-centered reason that this ministry needs to exist. It will answer the "why" question. A clear purpose statement will help you make sense of your program, use volunteers more effectively, and provide direction for growth and development for all Daughters of Imani. Your purpose statement should be simple and meaningful. In developing the purpose statement, answer the following questions:

Δ Why is this program necessary?
Δ What is the need it will meet?

DEVELOPING A MISSION STATEMENT
Once the "why" question is answered, the new question will be "How?" How will we accomplish what God has called us to do? It is now time to develop a mission statement. A mission statement is a very brief paragraph or statement that describes what will be accomplished. A mission statement is developed to guide the work and activities through implementation. An African proverb says, "If you don't know where you are going, any road will take you there." The mission statement is the decision about where you are going. It should be action oriented and compelling.

Once the direction has been decided, the goals and objectives become clearer. Examples of mission statements are as follows:

Δ To build a comprehensive faith-based program to address the spiritual needs of African-American youth.
Δ To provide female mentors to work with, guide, and assist young females on an individual basis to develop self-esteem, career goals, and academic excellence.

The Council of Women may brainstorm, with each person submitting examples and ideas of purpose and mission statements. Proverbs 15:22 states, "Without counsel, plans go wrong, but with many advisers they succeed." After collecting ideas from the women, one can be assigned to come up with statements that articulate the purpose and mission of your Daughters of Imani program. When the direction of the program has been set, make leadership decisions. Communicate with the entire group and decide who will occupy which positions. Feel free to negotiate roles based on the interest and availability of women.

After leadership positions have been decided, the Ohemma calls a Council of Women/Elders meeting to plan the entire Daughters of Imani program. The design of the program should cover one school year. The Administrative Team and the Council of Women/Elders should begin meeting in early summer to plan the following:

1. Organizing and training mentors
2. Recruiting girls and their parents
3. Having Introduction sessions for girls and their parents
4. Planning for all of the sessions

5. Planning for fields trips and informal activities
6. Planning for the Celebration Ritual and Banquet

The total Daughters of Imani program encompasses the following:

Δ 2–3 weeks of planning
Δ 6 weeks mentor training or 3 weekend retreats
Δ 3 weeks of coordinating girls and introductory sessions:
   a. Introductory meeting of girls and parents
   b. Mentor introductions and pairing with girls
   c. Girls and parents covenant signing meeting/Fall Open House

Δ Programming (one school year) of activities
   a. Length and timing of sessions will depend on age level, site schedule, and the availability of personnel. However, allow a minimum of two hours for each session.
   b. Circles should meet no fewer than twice a month.
   c. Bible study is a requirement. Bible study may be conducted as part of the circle meeting or at a separate time that can include girls not in the Daughters of Imani program.
   d. Field trips and special events may be scheduled in between sessions.
   e. Be open to opportunities that may arise, festivals, exhibits that come to town, and so forth.

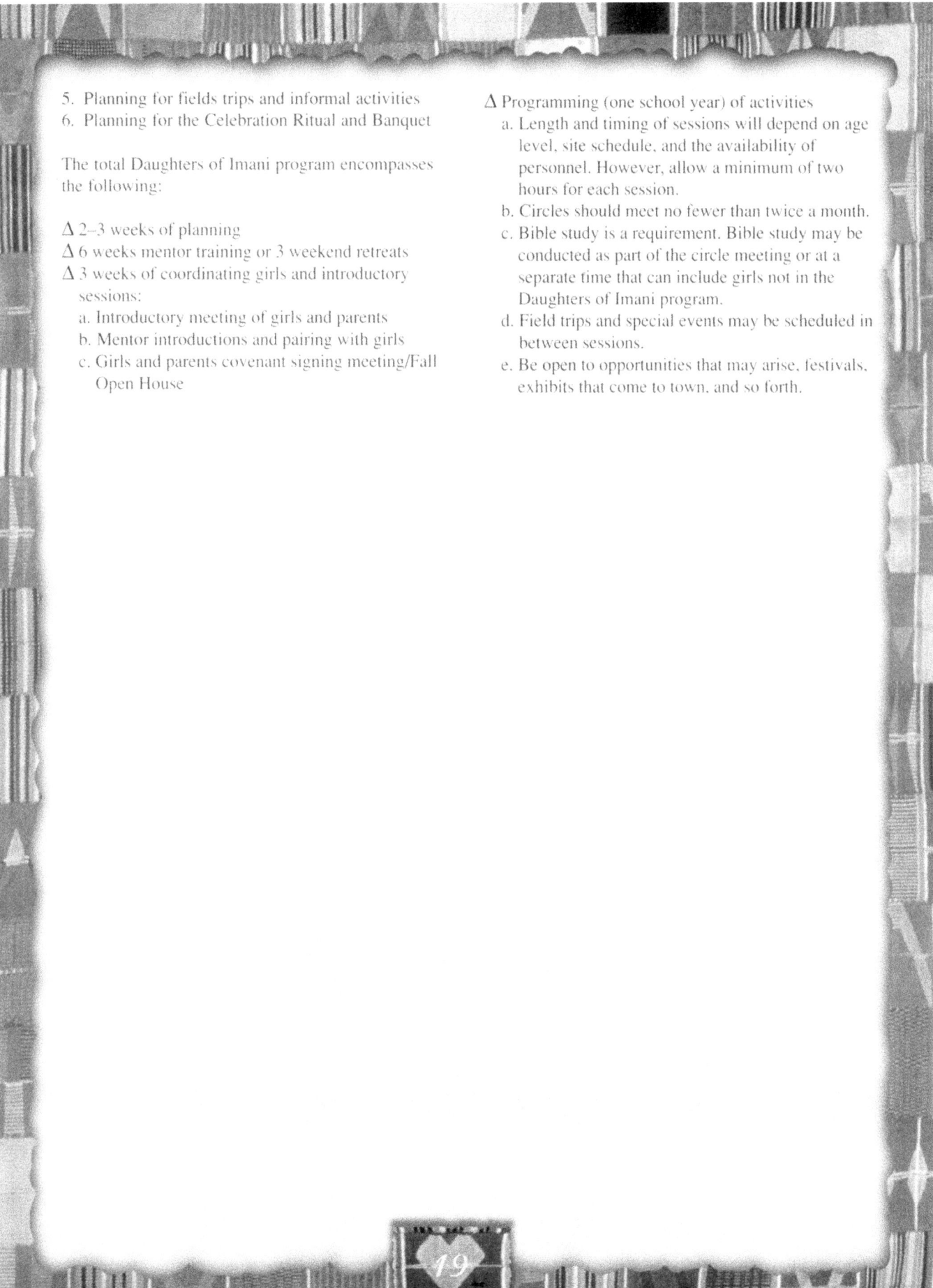

Chapter 4

MENTOR TRAINING

Mentoring is a one-to-one relationship over a prolonged period of time between a youth and older person. This relationship helps to provide consistent support, guidance, and assistance as the younger person goes through difficult or challenging situations or periods in life. The goal of mentoring is to help the younger person gain the skills and confidence to be responsible for her own future. Being a mentor is like being a friend, except that the mentor is the person with the most experience. Three components to the mentoring relationship mirror friendship. One is commitment; the mentor commits her time, energy, and wisdom to the participant. Reciprocity is another. This is perhaps one of the most important concepts in friendship, because relationships exemplify give and take. A relationship goes both ways. Our mentors are responsible for holding the participants accountable for reciprocity in the mentoring relationship. Intimacy is another aspect, creating a sacred space to share thoughts and experiences. However, intimacy does not mean that the mentor should inform the participant of all of her own problems. It means that the participant should feel safe enough to talk about her pain and struggle. It means that after trust is established, the participant can receive helpful advice and encouragement from her mentor.

A mentor should seek to become a friend to the participant. Mentor relationships may last a lifetime. The mentor should work actively with the knowledge of the girl's parents/family elder. Mentors participate with the girls in the sister circle, the large group, and occasionally one to one. It is recommended that mentors contact their protegees between meeting dates.

Mentoring has been a buzz word in today's society; however, mentoring is just as much a spiritual concept as it is a secular one. The Bible speaks to us about mentoring in Titus 2:3-5:

> Likewise, tell the older women to be reverent in behavior, not to be slanderers or slaves to drink; they are to teach what is good, so that they may encourage the young women to love their husbands, to love their children, to be self-controlled, chaste, good managers of the household, kind.

Other biblical examples of mentoring relationships include Moses and Joshua (Deuteronomy 3:23-29), Ruth and Naomi (Ruth 1:1-19), Eli and Samuel (1 Kings 19-19-21), Paul and Timothy (Acts 16:1-5), and Jesus and the disciples (Matthew 4:17-21). Elizabeth and Mary are another example, which will be more fully explored as the mentors do Bible study, as based on *Showing Mary: How Women Can Share Prayers, Wisdom, and the Blessings of God,* by Renita J. Weems. This book will help mentors better understand the mentoring relationship.

When you begin meeting with the women, engage them in discussion on issues that affect women. There may be a diversity of opinions concerning problems and solutions. The training sessions and content will provide a structure for the women to meet several times before working with youth, building group cohesiveness and solidarity. During the training, mentors are given guidelines and tools for working with girls and for participating in the overall program. Mentors are asked to practice the five Cs of mentoring—consistency, communication, commitment, candor, and caring.

MENTOR TRAINING SESSIONS

Mentor training may be provided in six consecutive meetings or in 3 weekend retreats. These meetings should include circle leaders, mentors, the administrative team, and all others who will interact in the Daughters of Imani program. All elders should become familiar with the basic format of the Daughters of Imani meetings with the youth. Training sessions that concern the curriculum should follow that pattern.

In preparation for the first training, all women participants in Daughters of Imani should take the time to read the book *Showing Mary: How Women Can Share Prayers, Wisdom, and the Blessings of God,* by Renita Weems. The chapters entitled "My Mother, My Self," "Shedding the Eternal Girl," "Midwives," "Showing," and "She Had No Children" are of particular importance in shedding light on the value and nature of mentoring relationships. These selections will constitute your first mentor training session. Each chapter is brief but filled with insights that can benefit potential mentors. Study questions can be found on the Internet at *www.walkworthypress.net/readshowingmary7.html.* These readings should help women clarify their desire and purpose as mentors. Training sessions include an overview of societal issues, an introduction to the Daughters of Imani program design, a focus on the needs of African-American girls, and sessions that focus on curriculum and praxis.

Daughters of Imani Meeting Format

The meeting format may have these components (allow a minimum of two hours for each training session):

Refreshments
Provide snacks for your meeting or something more substantial if you are using a retreat setting. Allow the women to eat and talk to get to know one another.

Introductions
In this part of the meeting, the women will introduce themselves to one another in a way that gives some insight as to who they are. The more bonded the women are, the more effective the work among the girls will be.

Worship and/or Bible Study (Use *Daughters of Imani: Young Women's Bible Study*)
Open the gathering with praise and prayer. Use music and engage the women in worship. This is a time to give thanks and remember family and ancestors who have paved the way for the freedoms Black people enjoy today. By using *Daughters of Imani: Young Women's Bible Study*, the women will understand how the two resources relate.

Presentation of Objectives of the Session

Training

Dialogue and Sharing

Closing Remarks
These remarks include summarizing the session's dialogue, emphasizing goals, praying together, and setting the agenda for the next meeting.

Daughters of Imani Circle Chant
The Daughters of Imani Circle Chant (page 23) should be performed at the ending of every Daughters of Imani related event. The first training session should include learning the Daughters of Imani Circle Chant. The chant is designed to evoke the concept of women surrounding and embracing women. The words of the chant represent meanings from several different African languages. All of the words describe an aspect of the Daughters of Imani woman.

Make a copy of the chant words for each participant so that she can practice the pronunciation and learn the meaning of the words. Practice the chant until all know it well.

The standard format for the Daughters of Imani Circle Chant is for all of the girls to create a circle by holding hands. The elder women—including the Ohemma, Elders, Mentors, and Helpers create another circle around the outside of the circle of girls. The result is a circle inside of a circle, symbolizing the elder women shielding and embracing the younger women.

During the training sessions, when the younger women are not present, the older women simply form one circle and chant the African words that declare that Daughters of Imani are faithful, gifted, queenly, filled with life, and beautiful women of God. The words are chanted in the African languages of Swahili, Ibo, and Yoruba. Swahili is spoken in much of Eastern Africa. Ibo is spoken in Nigeria. Yoruba is spoken both in Nigeria and Benin, West African countries. The chants will help to create a bond of sacredness and unity among the women. Arm movements made while holding hands will demonstrate power, growth, connectedness, and development.

Daughters of Imani Circle Chant Words

Imani (ee-MAH-nee) "faithful" (Swahili)
Isoke (ee-SHAW-keh) "gifted" (Yoruba)
Malika (mah-LEE-kah) "queenly" (Swahili)
Aisha (ah-EE-shah) "filled with life" (Swahili)
Naima (nah-EE-mah) "gracious" (Swahili)
Ifeoma (ee-FAY-oh-MAH) "beautiful" (Ibo)

Daughters of Imani Circle Chant

Directions

1. Girls hold hands, forming a circle
2. Women hold hands, forming a circle around girls
3. All hands remain held throughout, except when saying, "Women of God!"

Chant

Daughters of Imani! (*Hands are down.*)

Isoke! (*Hands are raised up.*)

Malika! (*Hands are down.*)

Aisha! (*Hands are raised up.*)

Naima! (*Hands are down.*)

Ifeoma! (*Hands are raised up.*)

Women of God! (*Hands are released and held up in praise to God; heads are lifted up in reverence to God.*)

TRAINING 1 (SHOWING MARY)
Objectives
   a. To begin a process of studying and planning together
   b. To help the women understand the nature of the mentoring relationship
   c. To learn the Circle Chant

TRAINING 2
Objectives
   a. To begin to build a sense of group identity and common purpose among the women
   b. To introduce the issues facing Black girls in the community, and begin to define the problems that must be addressed
   c. To establish a dialogical format to frame ongoing discussions

Group Dialogue
Get to know one another and the issues that affect the development of Black women. The goal of Daughters of Imani is to teach Black girls what it means to be African-American women spiritually, culturally, and physically. Before your group begins talking about the girls with whom you will be working, the participants need to talk about their own experiences as African-American women. Begin the discussion by asking these questions and inviting each woman to answer:

Δ How are Black women portrayed in American society today?
Δ How important is self-image?
Δ How do Black women work to overcome negative messages?
Δ Describe one way you have experienced racism or sexism. How did you deal with it?
Δ What do you feel are some critical issues facing young Black girls today?

Introduce the problem-solving format you will be using in various discussions. Write out these questions for the group to see. Keep the list for future discussions.

Δ What is the problem?
Δ What causes it?
Δ What are possible solutions?
Δ How do we implement the solution?

Your group will spend the next training sessions working through these questions as a foundation for continuing dialogue about the needs of Black girls. This way of addressing problems is logical and clear, yet it is flexible and allows for group dynamics to develop. This process provides a structure for the women to have a dialogue and to struggle together with these issues. Questions for group discussion:

Δ What are the problems facing Black girls in American society? in the community?
Δ What underlying causes lead to these problems?
Δ Think of some clear and effective solutions that may be applied to these problems.
Δ How can we, as African-American women, implement these solutions?

Struggle as a group with the answers or non-answers. Don't settle for pat and easy solutions. Dig into the matter and examine the issues deeply. This discussion—hard work as it may be—is nevertheless a valuable time for your group of women and talk about their convictions as well as their experiences.

TRAINING 3 (Part A)
Objectives
   a. To introduce the women to the basic principles of and philosophy behind the Daughters of Imani rites of passage program
   b. To reflect on the problems facing Black girls in American society through the discussion of statistical data and considering appropriate interventions
   c. To give the women a sense of the importance of their commitment to and presence in the lives of Black girls

Icebreaker
Have the women sit in a circle. Have each woman take a turn introducing herself to the group and making an "I am" statement about herself (for example: "I am a mother." "I am a lawyer.") Continue until each one has made ten statements. This exercise will give your group insights as to how each woman perceives herself.

Group Dialogue
Use the handouts to expose the women to the issues and to promote discussion. Explore with the mentors the issues of the need for commitment and consistency by Black women working with Black girls. Encourage them to consider carefully their

involvement in the Daughters of Imani program, and challenge them to invite other women to become involved. Women need to acknowledge and experience the urgency that faces urban Black girls and their communities. It is not a light task to take on the responsibility of mentoring and serving as a role model. Half-hearted involvement of a woman who has not thought through her commitment may have a devastating impact on the life of a young girl. Don't ask for commitments yet, but start the women thinking.

Distribute the Trends for Urban African American Females handout (page 29) then the Age-Level handout (page 30).

After discussing these items, the group is ready to talk about the overall goals and objectives for a Daughters of Imani program. Review the Vision, Mission, Purpose and Theology statements in Chapter 1. All mentors must come to understand that Daughters of Imani exists to teach Black girls what it means to be African-American women spiritually, culturally, socially, emotionally, and physically. These dimensions of self are explored in order to help participants develop a strong self-image and self-esteem by knowing who they are in Christ. At this point, you will also define the methods and procedures by which the Daughters of Imani program addresses the needs of Black female youth. The goals of the program will be met through a two-pronged approach:

First, Christian African-American women will engage the girls in personal relationships and thus model and teach womanhood that is both African American and Christian.

Second, the Daughters of Imani curriculum will provide a format and structure to encourage the interactive involvement of the women with the girls as well as content about being a Christian, African-American woman.

TRAINING 3 (Part B)
(If most of these women participated in the initial visioning of the program [pages 17–19] in which motivation was discussed, you may choose to go directly to Training 4.)

Objectives
a. To identify some of the specific needs of Black girls
b. To discuss viable solutions as to how those needs may be met and for the women see themselves as a group implementing one or some of those solutions
c. To recognize the power of the Christian gospel for meeting the needs of Black girls

Icebreaker
Before the meeting, prepare index cards or small pieces of paper with the name of a famous or historical African-American woman on each. Prepare one card for each of the women in your group. Affix a card to each woman's back as she enters the room, instructing the women not to tell one another what name is on their card. When each woman has a name on her back, the women must mingle and ask one another questions to guess what name they have. Limit the time, or limit the number of questions to ten.

Group Dialogue
A. Ask the women to put together a list of negative influences that have an impact on the girls of the community. Ask the women to speak openly and honestly about their impressions of resources that they have reviewed on Black girls and women. Not all of the women will think alike or agree on all issues. However, through open dialogue, your group can come to an agreement on how to work together to address the needs of Black girls in your community. Discuss the issues that point to the need for programs like Daughters of Imani.

Δ How can Black women respond to these issues?
Δ How can Black women respond to the crises facing Black girls?
Δ Do Black women have any obligation to respond to the crises mentioned?

These are all questions to which there are no immediate or automatic answers. These are questions for your group to struggle with in developing a group identity, common goals, and motivation. Struggling together in order to know what you are about and what you desire to accomplish is a key to the group's effectiveness.

B. Ask the women to examine their personal motives for wanting to be involved in a program such as Daughters of Imani. There is no wrong answer. Each woman has different and personal reasons. Each woman represents different experiences that have led her to this point. Recognize, however, and affirm the shared experiences of racism and sexism in your group. List the various motives for participating in Daughters of Imani, which may include family, children, self, community, religion, among others. As you articulate among yourselves your struggles as Black women, attempt to identify common positive measures of coping and pursuing your goals in the face of opposition.

C. As a Christian rites of passage program, Daughters of Imani affirms that Jesus Christ is key to coping with struggles. Christians often state that Jesus is the answer to any problem. How is Christ the answer to the crises facing Black girls and the Black community? As issues arise in the next few months, work at all of them from a Christian perspective; but be real and don't offer fake or insubstantial solutions. Struggle with each need. Pray together, read the Word, ask a pastor or spiritual leader for help.

TRAINING 4
Objectives
 a. To assist the women in communicating the philosophy and practices of the Daughters of Imani program
 b. To review the Daughters of Imani mentor helps and rituals

Icebreaker
Have the women gather into a circle and stretch out one hand to reach across and grab the hand of a person across from them. Ask them to use the other hand to join with someone else in the circle. Be sure that no one is holding both hands with the same person. The task is now for the group to untangle itself without releasing one another's hands.

A. Have copies of the statements of Mission and Purpose that were developed by the Council of Women. These and the Mentor Helps handout (page 32) will assist mentors in describing the program to others.

B. Distribute copies of Working With Girls handout (page 33). Talk about the six keys listed there. Ask the women to provide examples from their own lives of how to live out those principles. Encourage storytelling. Affirm the fact that no one does these things perfectly; but that with God's help, the women will find their efforts bearing fruit.

C. Talk about the steps the girls take for becoming and remaining members of Daughters of Imani. Refer the women to the Mentor Covenant (page 31), the Pledge (page 48), Affirmations (page 49–50), and the Code of Conduct (page 51). You may want to provide loose-leaf notebooks for the mentors so that they can assemble the papers into a handbook. Go through the notebook page by page, allowing the women to familiarize themselves with the material.

D. Use the chapter on rituals (Chapter 7, page 41) to help mentors become familiar with ceremonies beyond the Daughters of Imani Chant (page 23).

TRAINING 5
Objectives
 a. To discuss the components of a Daughters of Imani meeting and other programming
 b. To familiarize the women with the Daughters of Imani curriculum

Icebreaker
In the spirit of continuing to build strong connections within your group, the women will play a toilet paper game. Bring rolls of toilet paper; pass a roll around the group, asking each person to take as much as she thinks she will need for the day. When everyone has taken some, tell the women that for each square of toilet paper they have, they must tell the group something about themselves. (Be sure not to waste the toilet paper by throwing it away.)

Group Dialogue
A. Distribute handouts of the Daughters of Imani Meeting Format (page 22). Review the material and discuss each component of the typical meeting structure. Emphasize the specific purpose of each part of the meeting. Create a planning chart or schedule that includes circle time, field trips, and special events. Now is the time for women to decide with what grade level they will work and to think about lessons on which they can take or find leadership. Every circle leader should have a planning guide.

B. Examine the Curriculum Overview (pages 58–59). Carefully review and discuss the goals for each unit and the focus for each lesson.

C. Talk about the chapter on Other Components (page 38). Discuss field trip possibilities, optional activities, Sisters of Niara activities, and a Journey Toward Womanhood retreat. Mentors, Circle Leaders, and coordinators will have the responsibility of reminding participants and parents about permission forms, emergency contact information, and public decorum. Mentors will also have the privilege of helping to debrief these experiences with the girls, what they found interesting or challenging about the trip or the activity.

TRAINING 6
Objectives
    a. To plan one session for Daughters of Imani participants
    b. To carry out and role play one session
    c. To benefit from observation of other elders

A. Women should divide into circles according to the grade level they are leading. Circle Leaders may have already met together and filled in the planning chart. Each group should choose either the first lesson they want to do or one that may give them difficulty in order to become more comfortable with the subject matter. Each group should also be prepared with appropriate materials.

B. Other elders will act as the participants as school-grade/age-level Circle Leaders carry out their lesson plan. These will be abbreviated sessions. Opening and Closing Rituals (pages 46 and 47, respectively) should be done at beginning and end of an entire meeting. The focus is on helping Circle Leaders and other presenters to be age appropriate in the lessons and activities they are presenting. Use the Daughters of Imani meeting format.

C. Between each presentation, allow time for those not leading to offer affirmations, suggestions, and information. Any critique should be given in love, in a spirit of partnership, and with the best interest of the girls at heart.

D. At the end of this meeting (retreat), the Ohemma should lead all Mentors, Elders, and Circle Leaders in a ritual that celebrates the end of this portion of the training. (See Chapter 7: Rituals, Pledges, and Ceremonies.) Those in leadership positions should realize that training is constant and should be willing to share information throughout the entire process, whether formally or informally. Each mentor should fill in and sign her Mentor Covenant (page 55).

Helpful Hints for All Leaders
In order to engage the young women and help them truly appreciate and enjoy the program, the following tips are provided:

1. Give awards for meeting the requirements at various stages of achievement. At the end of the year, each Daughter of Imani receives a certificate of achievement. The girls receive one gold seal on their certificate for each month they have successfully completed their activities. Consider giving awards for attendance.
2. Develop awards that celebrate growth and positive behavior. Present the awards during the meetings. Give concrete approval to participants who refuse to give in to negative peer pressure or to engage in violence in a certain situation. Give awards to girls who make the academic honor roll. These unexpected awards provide incentive to the other girls to do what is right and self-affirming.
3. Create T-shirts, sweatshirts, hats, and so forth. Use these items to help provide a positive group identity for daughters of Imani (Elders and girls). Encourage participants to wear them not only for Daughters of Imani events and activities but also at school, home, and among their peers out in the neighborhood. These items may also function as awards.
4. Mentors may assist their protegees in keeping their portfolios. Help the girls keep track of projects and assignments. Remind them of what needs to be done. Do not do any work for them, but encourage them to meet every goal.

It is also a good idea for Mentors to create a sample presentation for each project listed in the planning guide. Seeing an example of the various projects will help spark the creativity of the participants and help them to understand what they are to do.

Visioning Self-Worth and Self-Esteem
    Adinkra Declarations of Self Esteem

Endurance and Bonding/Family Matters
    Family Tree
    Who Is Family? Mixed-Media Collage
    Prayer Bracelets
    That's My Sister Heritage Project

Health and Sexuality
    HIV/AIDS Peer Education Tool

DAUGHTERS OF IMANI MEETING FORMAT

Opening Ritual With Prayer and Praise (page 46)

Celebration of Women
Circles may rotate the responsibility of this community presentation. The circles will do a creative presentation concerning the life of women. The circle leader may use a small team of other women and some girls, no more than 3–5 people, who will prepare ahead of time for the presentation. The team may use excerpts from appropriate literary works, music, art, skits, and so on. Each lesson will have suggestions, but the leader may feel free to choose. The suggested women tend to relate in some way to the focus of each lesson.

Lesson Focus
All presenters should prepare for the session by reading the lesson focus. Participants may also be interested in hearing some of these instructional essays. The activities in each lesson are quite varied. The lesson focus should help tie together and bring out the purpose of all discussions and activities.

Bible Study
Leaders should use lessons from the *Daughters of Imani: Young Women's Bible Study* component. This section may occur with a large group or in small groups. It may be eliminated if a separate session for Bible study that participants are required to attend is preferred.

Small Groups
There are at least two activities to be experienced in age-level groupings. Elders are responsible for adjusting the material, depending on the age level of their circle participants. If Activity 2 has been combined with Griot Time (usually for the community quilt) age levels will meet together.

Activity 1

Activity 2

Griot (GREE-oh) Time
In her book *Racism 101*, Nikki Giovanni insists that "There always must be griots." This how we know who we are and from whence we have come. *Griot* is a French word that describes the role of historian/storyteller in Senegal, a French-speaking African country. Persons who fulfill this role are found in most African cultures. At gatherings, griots colorfully relate to the community facts, poetry, songs, and stories concerning the values and history of the people. For Griot Time, invite a Mentor or Elder to speak concerning the listed topic.

Closing Ritual (page 47)

Trends for Urban African-American Females

The decisions that we make during our adolescent years can be important in shaping the direction that our lives may take. Studies have shown that many inner city teens, facing the daily challenges of living in low-resource and high-risk communities, are at a disadvantage.

Low-income African-American adolescent females need extensive support for developing and implementing career plans. Many reside in economically depressed inner cities where access to decent schools and opportunities for employment are severely limited. Thus they may lack academic skills and career-related experiences and may perceive narrow career opportunities for themselves, which combine to pose formidable obstacles to obtaining future jobs or careers.

It is critical to help young low-income minority women understand and overcome the effects of perceived barriers and negative outcomes on their own beliefs in their career abilities, interests, and goals. They need to build skills to identify racism, sexism, and discrimination; and to develop effective coping strategies for dealing with discrimination and social barriers that can limit their career and educational development and participation.

African-American girls are over-represented in the criminal and juvenile justice systems at alarming rates. They are also more likely than all other youth to be victimized by violence. According to the 1999 National Crime Victimization Survey data, the violent victimization rate for female, African-American youth was almost double the rate for female, White youth and about 25 percent greater than the rate for male African-American and White teens. Moreover, the violent victimization rate for younger African-American girls ages 12–15 exceeded the rate for African-American girls ages 16–19 by more than one-third.

There are serious educational achievement gaps facing African-American students. According to the Michigan State Department of Education, African-American students are at the bottom of the scale in reading, mathematics and science. They continue to lag behind Caucasians, Asians, and other ethnic groups. This pattern is said to begin as early as fourth grade. African-American students seldom recover from this educational deficit.

Examine these national trends. Try to discover underlying causes. Discuss the effect of institutional racism on the Black community and on Black females in particular. Also look at how African-American people have responded to the problems. Emphasize positive and creative solutions already existing in the Black community through national or local initiatives.

Permission is granted to the purchaser to photocopy this page for use with DAUGHTERS OF IMANI: A CHRISTIAN RITES OF PASSAGE FOR AFRICAN-AMERICAN YOUNG WOMEN, © 2005 by Abingdon Press. All rights reserved.

Age-Level Development

Elementary-age children of younger and younger ages are exposed to more and more mature issues through negative environments, media, and peer groups. Degrading images of women in TV shows, movies, and music videos have an especially negative impact. Proactive measures with young children will yield significant fruit in the lives of urban girls. This age group is characterized by growth in height, the first pubic hairs and budding of the breast, and reproductive system development. Menstruation usually begins. Thinking is less concrete and more symbolic, philosophical, more abstract. Younger adolescents can't always make clear connections between decisions and their consequences. These girls are preoccupied with themselves; they are self-absorbed but also have a lowered self-esteem. The girls begin to redefine family relationships, and they branch out socially and emotionally. Peers become very important, because being around them helps to reassure the girls that others share similar changes. Sexuality is a topic of interest to these girls.

Mid-Adolescence (between the ages of 13–17)
Young people of middle school experience inordinate stress and pressure in dealing with issues among their peer group, such as crime, violence, sexuality, and drugs. Dysfunctional family and hostile neighborhood environments contribute to the vulnerability of their persons. This age group is characterized by reaching usually the physical height that she will remain for the rest of her life. Body fat increases around the hips, thighs, calves, and breast; pubic hair grows; pelvic area increases. The girl begins to look more womanly. She has increased abstract thinking, understanding of decisions and consequences. The mid-adolescent girl begins to feel more comfortable as a woman and wonders who she will be and what her life will be like. She often disagrees with parents over who is in control and draws closer to peers through a selective process. She may increasingly test her ability to attract members of the opposite sex, and may experiment with what defines the borders of her sexual behavior.

Late Adolescence (between the ages of 17–20)
This is a crucial time in development for young Black girls. There is a need for focus on leadership development, spiritual discipleship, college preparation, or work readiness. Opportunities must be given for leadership development. These opportunities include problem-solving situations and involvement in planning activities. Girls should be encouraged to make plans and set goals for their career choices at this age. College trips and vocational experiences will stimulate their vision for what they can achieve in life. Provide exposure to various vocational trades that may interest the youth. This age group is characterized by growth in height and more body fat. Important intellectual development takes place. They take the opportunity to gain mastery over complex thinking. More emotional and social growth comes along with the urge to define themselves. Family relationships sometimes seem unimportant. The girls become more sophisticated socially and emotionally. Their relationships with peers may now be about helping to reinforce their values, instead of discovering what those values are. At this point, the girls also know what they want in terms of sexuality.

Permission is granted to the purchaser to photocopy this page for use with DAUGHTERS OF IMANI: A CHRISTIAN RITES OF PASSAGE FOR AFRICAN-AMERICAN YOUNG WOMEN, © 2005 by Abingdon Press. All rights reserved.

Daughters of Imani
Mentor Covenant

I agree to uphold the principles of love, joy, peace, and the good news of faith and salvation that come from the teachings and resurrection of Our Lord and Savior Jesus Christ.

I agree to embody in my spirit and personhood an attitude of nurture, support, and community in the Daughters of Imani program.

I agree to mentor at least one girl, which entails spending time with her no fewer than once a month, developing a relationship with her and her family, and becoming a woman whom she can look up to for wisdom and insight.

I agree to attend all Daughters of Imani programs as I am able, and to interact with the small-group learning activities workshops that the girl I mentor belongs to, strengthening the bond with her and with the other girls and mentors in the small group.

Signed _____ Date _____

Permission is granted to the purchaser to photocopy this page for use with **DAUGHTERS OF IMANI: A CHRISTIAN RITES OF PASSAGE FOR AFRICAN-AMERICAN YOUNG WOMEN**, © 2005 by Abingdon Press. All rights reserved.

Mentor Helps

PURPOSE OF DAUGHTERS OF IMANI
Daughters of Imani is an African-American mentoring program designed to help young girls experience and work through the rites of passage to becoming a woman. The group addresses spiritual, emotional, and social needs; and deals with issues such as personal hygiene, work habits, self-concepts and self-esteem, knowledge of African-American heritage and culture, and education. The purpose of the curriculum is to involve girls in positive interaction with African-American women in preparation for adolescence and adulthood.

GOAL OF DAUGHTERS OF IMANI
The goal of Daughters of Imani is to teach African-American girls what it means to be African-American women spiritually, culturally, socially, emotionally, and physically. These five dimensions of self are explored thoroughly in order to infuse the girls with a strong self-image and with self-esteem as a result of knowing who they are in Christ. The basic method by which this goal will be met is to provide Christian, African-American women to engage the girls in personal relationships and thus model and teach Black womanhood and what it means to be an African-American Christian. The Daughters of Imani curriculum provides a format and structure to develop this dynamic.

PHILOSOPHY OF DAUGHTERS OF IMANI
The Daughters of Imani mentoring program addresses the experience of Black girls from the holistic perspective of Christian ministry.

The Daughters of Imani curriculum explores and affirms the innate spirituality and moral fiber of African-American culture. It provides positive experiences and dialogue about African-American culture, heritage, and traditions. The Daughters of Imani group examines issues of female adolescence and puberty, addressing everything from etiquette to sexuality. Daughters of Imani provides an affirming atmosphere in which to examine the social and emotional aspects of daily life peculiar to the experience of Black females.

Daughters of Imani operates from three premises for mentors:

1. That Black girls can see a better life for themselves in the example of their mentors.
2. That Black girls will be drawn to positive, nurturing, self-assured Black women who show a genuine interest in them.
3. That Black girls will be more than equipped not only to survive but thrive in life as they learn and embrace who they are in Christ.

Daughters of Imani creates a medium for Black girls to receive instruction from positive Black women, resulting in lives of realized potential and personal satisfaction. Daughters of Imani's methodology is to put nurturing Black women in a position to teach young Black girls, for the purpose of instilling hope for who they can be. Daughters of Imani's goal is to cultivate and develop the inner person. Through actively engaging the curriculum, the young persons will internalize positive Christian beliefs about who they are in the world and their inherent values so that the girls will gain and possess inner peace and strength to bring to bear on their external situation, whatever it might be.

Permission is granted to the purchaser to photocopy this page for use with DAUGHTERS OF IMANI: A CHRISTIAN RITES OF PASSAGE FOR AFRICAN-AMERICAN YOUNG WOMEN, © 2005 by Abingdon Press. All rights reserved.

Working With Girls

Use this list as a guide for developing relationships with the girls.

1. Build Relationship
The relationships that develop between the mentors and the girls are at the core of the Daughters of Imani program. Through formal and informal interaction with positive African-American women, African-American girls will get a glimpse into what Black womanhood is about. The group will meet for a while before matching girls and women with each other. Those match-ups might develop naturally. After a time, some of the girls and women will be drawn to each other. The foundation of the mentor-protegee relationship is a friendship. Being a friend and sharing your life is the basis of what being a mentor is all about.

2. Be Yourself
It is important not to enter into relationships with girls by trying to be something we are not. Children and youth respect honesty and realness. Young people sometimes test an adult's sincerity or commitment to the relationship in a variety of ways. Acting out with bad behavior or shocking the person with their language or attitudes are ways some young people will test boundaries to see how and if an adult will correct or admonish them.

Never match bad behavior and never offer money for good behavior. Remember that positive reinforcement through verbal affirmation and encouragement or special incentives is an effective way to influence behavior. Genuine caring and concern are the qualities that win over young people.

3. Spend High-Quality Time Together
Include your protegee in your family circle. While children feel loyalty to their own families, they enjoy extending their family circle and seeing ways of relating that may mirror their own families or be markedly different. Never compare families or give the impression that yours is better. Such statements will lead to resentment and contempt. Time spent does not have to cost a lot of money. Consider the following: preparing a meal, doing some everyday shopping, going to a movie, watching a TV show and discussing it, doing hair and nails, and so on.

4. Set an Agenda for Conversation
Be prepared with an agenda or something to talk about. Engage the girl in talking about her life, her family, her school, or a particular problem in her life. Consider beforehand what you might want to discuss, but be flexible enough to let things flow. Be ready to listen and observe. Even when kids are not talkative, you can learn something about them by how they dress, conduct themselves, act around their peers, and act around you. Young people will open up to an adult who is genuinely interested in what they have to say. You may need to set it aside, but having an agenda ensures that your time together will be constructive.

5. Engage the Parents and/or Other Appropriate Family Members
Parent involvement is critical. Take time to sit down with the parents and discuss the progress of the girls in Daughters of Imani. Make visits to home every now and then. For the mentors, picking up girls and dropping them off at home afterward are natural times to meet and get to know the family of your protegee.

6. Work on a Joint Project
During this period of time, the young woman with a mentor identifies a project reflecting an interest she will present to the community on the day of the ceremony. Examples of projects are musical composition or performance, art, poetry, cooking. The youth are also responsible for keeping a journal, reading specific books and writing short reviews, interviewing family elders and community leaders, and completing a community service project. Help your protegee stay on target with her portfolio.

Map of Africa

West Africa

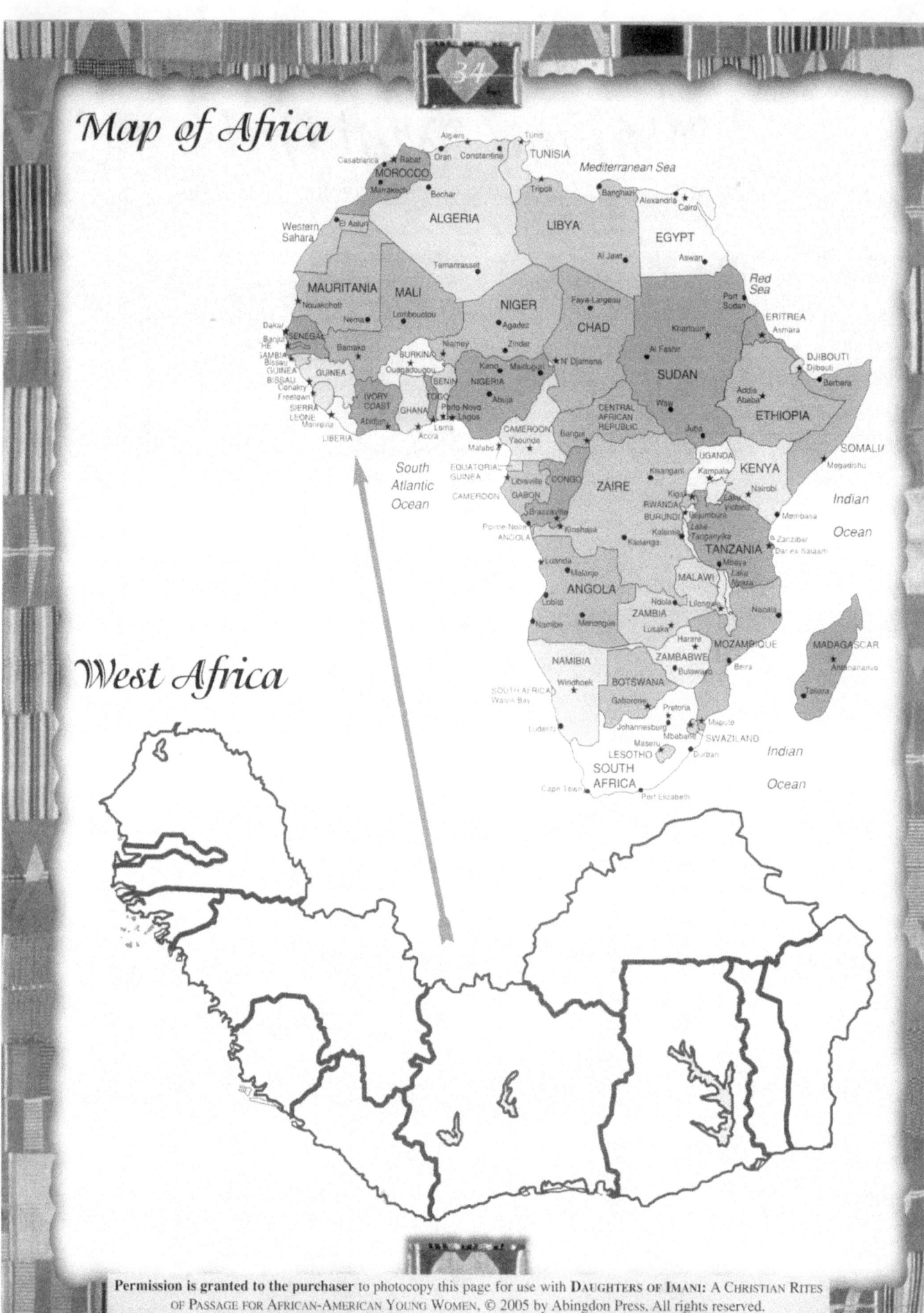

Permission is granted to the purchaser to photocopy this page for use with DAUGHTERS OF IMANI: A CHRISTIAN RITES OF PASSAGE FOR AFRICAN-AMERICAN YOUNG WOMEN, © 2005 by Abingdon Press. All rights reserved.

Chapter 5

MEMBERSHIP

ELIGIBILITY

All young ladies between the ages of 8 and 18 are invited to complete a membership application. There are three categories of membership—standard members, initiates, and Sisters of Niara (nee-YAH-rah). *Niara* is a Swahili word that means "of high purpose." All members may also be referred to as "Daughters." The Daughters of Imani program engages young African-American females from elementary through high school age. Daughters of Imani are divided into three school-level small groups: elementary, middle school and high school. Small groups engage in learning activities and some Bible study activities in order to account for the developmental differences among young women as they face certain issues and also prepare for certain periods in their lives. The Daughters of Imani program activities come together for large group activities as well—Griot testimonies, games, and worship.

Youth enter the program through an application process in which they are interviewed with their parent(s) or a family elder and learn the expectations of a Daughters of Imani member. Both the girls and their parents are asked to sign the application to make a commitment for consistent involvement.

Standard membership is open to any young lady between the ages of 8 and 18. A standard member is one who seeks to build character, self-esteem, and relationships with others of like interests.

An initiate is one who is 16 years old and is preparing to cross over into the threshold of young adulthood. Initiates are those who, at the conclusion of the program year during their sixteenth year of existence, have the opportunity to move to a higher level of social growth and development. To be considered for graduation from Daughters of Imani, initiates must complete a thematic portfolio and a comprehensive examination. After graduation, initiates are encouraged to return and serve as Mentors or Sister Circle Leaders.

A Sister of Niara is an initiate who is chosen by the adult leadership because she demonstrates or has expressed a desire to develop leadership skills. This member is seeking a more meaningful relationship with God and will actively participate in the Imani/Niara School of Servant Leadership. It is an additional component in which initiates may participate. Each participant commits to applying the seven challenges of purpose to their daily lives. The seven challenges are based on Mark 12:30-31:

You shall love the Lord your God with all your heart, and with all of your soul, and with all of your mind, and all of your strength . . . love your neighbor as yourself.

The seven challenges of purpose are:

Challenge 1—Commit to spend daily quiet time with God

Challenge 2—Commit your mind to God

Challenge 3—Commit to participate in youth Bible study

Challenge 4—Commit to friendships that hold each other accountable

Challenge 5—Commit to a Lifestyle of Worship and living that pleases God

Challenge 6—Commit to Honor Your Parents

Challenge 7—Commit to Your Church and Your Youth Group

The Sisters of Niara activities include monthly leadership meetings and a summer retreat. Sisters of Niara are also given the responsibility of assisting with operation of the Daughters of Imani ministry. For example, the Sisters may have the responsibility of taking attendance, typing the newsletter, calling absent members, sending notes to absent members, leading the praise dance at meetings, and calling mentors to remind them of their commitment. Skills development includes leading a meeting and learning how to communicate effectively orally and in writing. The Sisters are challenged to help others who are less fortunate. It may be best for this component to be added to the program when the program is in its second year.

MEMBERSHIP REQUIREMENTS

As with membership with any group or organization, there are membership requirements. Daughters of Imani membership requirements include the following:

1. Regular attendance and participation at study retreats/regular sessions;
2. Completion of individual and group assignments;

3. Adhering to the Code of Conduct; and
4. Participation in fundraising efforts.

All participants are encouraged to be members in good standing. Members in good standing are those who attend 75 percent of the scheduled study retreats, complete work as assigned, adhere to the Code of Conduct, and participate in fundraising efforts. Persons who participate sporadically and half-heartedly will not have the privilege of attending cultural arts excursions or retreats.

Upon being accepted into the program, participants may be divided into groups according to the grade levels that work best for your community. While standard members, initiates, and Sisters of Niara are expected to exhibit differing levels of leadership and responsibility, all girls will participate in workshops and activities together.

SURVIVAL KIT

Each participant will need a survival kit that must be brought to each study retreat. The Survival Kit may include the following:

Δ Bible (*Extreme Faith Bible: Contemporary English Version*, published by the American Bible Society may be available at reduced prices)
Δ portfolio
Δ *The Real Deal: A Spiritual Guide for Black Teen Girls*, by Billie Montgomery Cook (Judson Press, 2004; ISBN: 0817014586)
Δ spiral notebook for note-taking and assignments
Δ journal
Δ writing instrument
Δ *Prayers That Avail Much for Teens*, by Germaine Copeland (Harrison House, 2003; ISBN: 1577946006) may also be included.

Each item in the survival kit serves a purpose. **The Bible** is the Word of God; it serves as a lamp unto our feet and a light for our path as we journey toward womanhood. **The journal** is where participants will their record thoughts, prayers, and progress on the journey. **The portfolio** will contain of notes, lessons, activities, and assignments. It will grow as the participant progresses in her growth and development. ***The Real Deal*** and ***Prayers That Avail Much for Teens*** offers spiritual support for a variety of situations as participants navigate their adolescence in relationship to God.

CEREMONIES

The Daughters of Imani year is marked by two ceremonies: the Opening Ceremony (pages 42–45) and the Crossing Over Ceremony (pages 53–54). Participants are required to attend both functions. The Opening Ceremony is the kick-off celebration to be done at the beginning of each Daughters of Imani year. At this time, new members are welcomed into the sisterhood. All participants should wear white, which is the color of innocence. Elders should wear purple, which denotes our royal heritage. The Opening Ceremony may take place during the Super Slumber Party or be incorporated in some other type of fellowship activity or meal.

The Crossing Over Ceremony ends the Daughters of Imani year. This ceremony signifies the crossing over of the initiates into the young adult community. During this year of participation in the program, initiates are held accountable for completing a portfolio or scrapbook, completing an open-book exam, and accomplishing certain tasks. Failure of any initiate to complete any of these assignments may jeopardize her crossing over. This ceremony presents the initiates to the community. Each initiate will share a talent with the community, leave a legacy for her little sisters, and read an essay on a designated topic. In addition, all initiates must give a corporate performance that demonstrates aspects of community. After individual presentations, each initiate will ask permission to enter the young adult community. The community will respond favorably, allowing the initiate to cross over.

In the case of an established Daughters of Imani program, some years may have no new members (Opening) or initiates (Closing). Adjust the ceremonies so that they still include sisterly bonding and opportunities that allow participants to share their gifts, talents, and learnings from the course of the year.

HONORING THE ELDERS

Each year at the closing program, honor the Elders within the community. Choose a "woman" to honor (the Honoree) by having participants nominate women who exemplify the characteristics they have been learning. Honoree(s) will be presented with an award or tribute of some kind. Honoring the Elders helps to broaden the support for this ministry throughout the community. Honorees may be inspired to become contributors, Mentors, instructors, or volunteers in upcoming years.

Chapter 6

OTHER COMPONENTS

THE FALL OPEN HOUSE

The Daughters of Imani program offers other components, the use of which may help you reach the goals you have for the young women in your community. Start the year with the Fall Open House. The Fall Open House is the annual recruitment event where the Council of Women spend a September Sunday afternoon or Friday evening introducing young ladies and their families to the Daughters of Imani ministry. Current members of Daughters of Imani invite their friends and family members to become a part of the ministry. Food, fun, and fellowship are the highlights of this event. The open house represents an opportunity for the high school members to serve as coordinators and agenda setters. After the first year, minimal adult leadership and help should be involved. One of the best ways to recruit and invite new members to join the program is for young people to see their peers as leaders.

THE SUPER SLUMBER PARTY

The Super Slumber Party is the event that initiates each program year. It is an evening where new participants are welcomed into the sisterhood through an evening of ceremony, celebration, fellowship, and learning about self and others. Conduct the Opening Ceremony (page 42–45) at this party and distribute the items for the Survival Kit (described on page 37). Help participants understand the meaning of the ceremony and the kit. This may also be a time for participants to review the Code of Conduct, the Pledge, and other items. Don't forget to plan other fun activities.

COMMUNITY QUILT

The making of a Community Quilt is an activity that will enable participants to create at least one project as a group, building fellowship and spanning the generations. Mentors should seek the wisdom and advice of a person who is knowledgeable in quilt-making for specific instructions. Mentors may even create a practice quilt during their own training. The girls should seek fabric pieces from relatives, friends, church members, and Daughters of Imani Elders. Each girl should classify her fabric pieces according to the giver, making note of the qualities that make this person beloved to her. Everything should be in order so that the group can begin working on the quilt by the fourth lesson of Unit 1. Elders/Mentors should determine the size of the groups as they work, understanding that all the pieces will be assembled into one large quilt that represents one year's work.

OUTINGS

Participants will have the opportunity to learn through **Field Trips** and **Cultural Arts Excursions**. Cultural Arts activities are a means of exposure to folk culture and fine arts. These activities give the young people a chance enhance their awareness of history, science, and the arts including different kinds of music, dance, theatre, visual art, and literature. The particular events will depend on what is offered locally. However, make the outings as diverse as possible.

Retreats will allow all daughters of Imani to set aside time for quiet thought, prayer and study. These gatherings help to build a spiritual foundation and enhance Christian character. By exposing young people to unfamiliar surroundings, they may be better able to focus and become open the power of the Holy Spirit and move toward a closer relationship with God.

SPECIAL EVENTS

You may also choose to do all or some of these special events, activities that provide participants additional opportunities to grow intellectually, physically, socially, emotionally, and culturally. Special Events may include Career Expo, Kwanzaa Celebration, Health Forum, Sports Lock In, and/or College Tour.

The Career Expo provides the participants the opportunity to meet with career professionals and participate in career education workshops that will assist them in planning for future careers.

Kwanzaa Celebration is a family affair where the principles of Kwanzaa are discussed, wisdom from the elders is imparted and the cultural arts are celebrated. African attire and traditional African and African-American dishes are served.

A Health Forum provides health and medical information specific to the needs of the participant population. Experiential learning opportunities, rap sessions, and health screenings may be available.

A Sports Lock-In is a structured recreational event that may take place at a local sports/recreational facility. Activities seek to provide fellowship that will fortify and strengthen sisterly bonding.

A College Tour provides an opportunity for the participants to visit a college campus. During their visit, participants will have the opportunity to dialogue and spend time with admissions representatives and members of the student body.

Outreach Events provide the participants the opportunity to serve as recruiters for the ministry. Invite potential members to outreach events to entice them to become a part of the Daughters of Imani ministry.

Leadership Development

The Daughters of Imani Program is intentional about Leadership Development. Leadership development covers the concepts and practices of leadership and encourages skills and assertiveness in attaining established goals. Each year, choose a group of middle school and high school students to participate in the Imani/Niara School of Servant Leadership.

All participants in this leadership component carry the title "Sisters of Niara" (see Membership Eligibility, page 36). These future leaders possess strong leadership abilities and have demonstrated a commitment to the vision of Daughters of Imani. This component allows the youth participants to experience a yearly leadership retreat and monthly meetings that enhance and develop their leadership skills. Throughout the course of the year, these participants are given the opportunity to further develop their leadership skills through exercising their call to leadership within the sisterhood and the neighboring community. The curriculum of the Imani/Niara School of Servant Leadership should be developed with the concepts below in mind:

A LEADER IS ...

△ **A LEADER'S WORK**—Leaders influence people toward a goal. While some leaders have more natural leadership abilities, all must develop their leadership skills. Help participants understand that they face the challenge of becoming the leader that God wants them to be.

△ **A LEADER'S CALLING**—Develop a lesson that explores the nature of a leader's call. For Christians, a call from God is life changing. When God calls you by name, you should listen. When God calls you to serve, you should obey. God has many ways of calling persons into leadership.

△ **A LEADER'S LIFESTYLE**—Develop a lesson that deals with character and integrity.

△ **A LEADER'S POWER**—With leadership comes power. Power has the potential to influence people for godliness. Develop a lesson that helps participants understand the positive and negative qualities of power.

△ **A LEADER'S STYLE**—A leader's style refers to her personal manner, unique behavior, or approach to leadership. Her style is a blend of her character, experiences, skills, limitations, and challenges. Even Christian leaders have weaknesses and failures. Develop a tool by which each participant can recognize her own style of leadership, along with her challenges and weaknesses.

△ **A LEADER'S TEAM**—Develop a lesson in which participants will be lead to understand that the work will be done more effectively and with greater ease as a team. Jesus illustrated the importance of teamwork in his own ministry, because God desires to work through many.

△ **A LEADER'S JOURNEY**—A Christian leader must always be willing to grow spiritually. Spiritual growth and development will enable her to better lead others and serve the Lord. Provide opportunities that will help Sisters of Niara to establish the priorities needed to ensure that they stay committed to the Lord.

△ **A LEADER'S LEGACY**—Each leader begins creating her legacy the day she begins serving in a leadership role. Encourage participants to think about these questions: What will you, the leader, leave behind? What convictions will you pass down? What will those you lead remember about you? It is important for a leader to determine what she wants her legacy to be before she begins to lead.

The culminating event of the year is the Journey Toward Womanhood Conference. This is time for the youth to assess their commitment to the program and begin to formulate goals for the upcoming year. It is also a time for quiet thought, reflection, prayer, and study.

Chapter 7

Rituals, Pledges, and Ceremonies

Daughters of Imani
A Journey Toward Womanhood
Opening Ceremony

This ceremony is to be used at the onset of the Daughters of Imani season. Youth participants are asked to wear white attire. Mentors, Elders and other volunteers are asked to wear purple or black. Make copies of pages 42–44 for Daughters of Imani leaders only. Make copies of the program on page 45 and the Daughters of Imani Pledge, page 48, for the Daughters and all others who are attending. Have a Survival Kit (see page 37) on hand for each youth participant. If possible, provide copies of the pledge to the initiates in advance of the ceremony so that they can begin to learn it.

GREETINGS
Ohemma: My sisters, my daughters, you have gathered in this assembly to take part in a very important ceremony. You are here today to follow in the footsteps of your ancestors and your sisters who have gone on before you. I welcome you.

INVITATION
Ohemma: I, the Ohemma, am pleased to invite you into membership in Daughters of Imani: A Journey Toward Womanhood.

When you were born, you came from your mother's womb into the light. At that time, you could do nothing on your own. You knew nothing. Someone had to take care of you. You had to be clothed, sheltered, raised, and instructed in the ways of life. The job was well done. You stand here today as proof. Again you are in darkness, for you know nothing of becoming a woman. Someone has to teach you, shelter you, and show you.

INTRODUCTION OF LEADERS
Ohemma: On the journey you are about to take, you will receive life and light and knowledge. On this journey, you will meet elders who are eager to instruct you. Listen now as the elders share important information with you.

Various Elders, Circle Leaders, and Mentors will read the next selections.
(Be sure to assign the selections ahead of time.)

THE ARTS
My daughters, you have come to increase your knowledge and appreciation of the creative arts in relationship to the history and culture of African people. We welcome you.

ASSERTIVENESS AND LEADERSHIP
My daughters, you have come to attain knowledge of how to be in control of your life and how to influence and gain the respect of others. You will become aware of the differences between assertive and aggressive behavior. We welcome you.

*Permission is granted to the purchaser to photocopy this page for use with **DAUGHTERS OF IMANI: A CHRISTIAN RITES OF PASSAGE FOR AFRICAN-AMERICAN YOUNG WOMEN**, © 2005 by Abingdon Press. All rights reserved.*

ENDURANCE AND BONDING

My daughters, you have come to participate in activities and engage in fellowship that will fortify sisterly bonding and physical, psychological, and spiritual endurance. We welcome you.

SOCIAL GRACE

My daughters, you have come to increase your knowledge and comfort in gracious social skills in meeting and greeting people of various groups as well as to develop skills in appropriate home entertaining. We welcome you.

HISTORY OF OUR PEOPLE

My daughters, you have come to celebrate and become more aware of the contributions of African and African-American women in leading the struggles of our people. We welcome you.

HUMAN SEXUALITY

My daughters, you have come to acquire knowledge and understanding of human sexuality, the physiological changes in the male and female bodies. You will learn how one's sexuality relates to responsibility, values, and respect for humanity. We welcome you.

HIV/AIDS AND OTHER SEXUALLY TRANSMITTED DISEASES

My daughters, you have come to learn how to honor your body as the temple of God's Spirit. You will heighten your knowledge and awareness of HIV/AIDS and other sexually transmitted diseases and the effects of each on the body and mind. We welcome you.

HOUSEKEEPING AND FINANCE

My daughters, you have come to attain knowledge of household cleanliness, repairs, and financial matters to enhance your knowledge of and skill as a creative and self-sufficient homemaker. We welcome you.

SELF-ESTEEM

My daughters, you have come to learn strategies to build positive self-esteem, using the Bible as a tool of affirmation. We welcome you.

TAKING CARE OF SELF

My daughters, you have come to enhance your knowledge and understanding of how physical appearance, mental attitude, and spiritual attitude interplay. You will learn how to and why you should keep yourself healthy through proper nutrition, exercise, and rest. We welcome you.

TIME MANAGEMENT AND ORGANIZATIONAL SKILLS

My daughters, you have come to attain knowledge of and skill in managing time, understanding, and completing tasks. We welcome you.

VALUES CLARIFICATION AND FUTURE PLANNING

My daughters, you have come to increase your knowledge and understanding of self by examining and clarifying your values as well as analyzing the importance of planning for the future.

PRESENTATION OF INITIATES

Ohemma: My daughters, you can see that the journey will be demanding, yet rewarding. It is important that you are instructed properly so that we will reach our goals.

To successfully complete your journey, you must begin to seek spiritual food for strength. Prayer, praise, and Bible study will heighten your conception and appreciation of how and why faith in God is a necessary part of your daily life.

My sisters, the following young ladies have come forth to seek admittance into the Daughters of Imani. I now present to you . . . (*Each participant is presented by name.*)

DAUGHTERS OF IMANI PLEDGE

Ohemma: My daughters, please recite with me the Daughters of Imani Pledge. (*Recite the Pledge.*)

PRESENTATION OF SURVIVAL KIT

Ohemma: We now present to each of you your Daughters of Imani Survival Kit: a Bible, portfolio, journal, and prayer book. Each serves a purpose. Each one is necessary.

The Bible is the Word of God. It is "a lamp unto [your] feet and a light unto [your] path." On your journey, hold God's Word in your heart that you might not sin against God.

Your portfolio contains activities and assignments to facilitate your growth and development.

Your journal allows you to record your thoughts and progress as you make your journey.

The prayer book will help you communicate with and get better acquainted with God.

PRAYER FOR THE JOURNEY

Ohemma: We welcome each of you into Daughters of Imani: A Journey Toward Womanhood. We pray that your journey will be rewarding and successful. Look to God for guidance and direction.

All: Dear God, we thank you for these young women who have come to make their journey toward womanhood. God, we pray that your Spirit will strengthen us and guide us. Help us be open to the knowledge you will reveal. Give us courage to stay on the journey. Give us love that we may grow and share together. Give us determination that we may stand on what we believe. Help us remain faithful to you. In Jesus' name, amen.

GOING FORTH

Ohemma: My sisters, you have now pledged membership into Daughters of Imani: A Journey Toward Womanhood. Let us greet one another.

Daughters of Imani
A Journey Toward Womanhood
Opening Ceremony

GREETINGS

INVITATION

INTRODUCTION OF LEADERS

PRESENTATION OF INITIATES

DAUGHTERS OF IMANI PLEDGE

PRESENTATION OF SURVIVAL KIT

PRAYER FOR THE JOURNEY

Ohemma: We welcome each of you into Daughters of Imani: A Journey Toward Womanhood. We pray that your journey will be rewarding and successful. Look to God for guidance and direction.

All: Dear God, we thank you for these young women who have come to make their journey toward womanhood. God, we pray that your Spirit will strengthen us and guide us. Help us be open to the knowledge you will reveal. Give us courage to stay on the journey. Give us love that we may grow and share together. Give us determination that we may stand on what we believe. Help us remain faithful to you. In Jesus' name, amen.

GOING FORTH

Daughters of Imani
Opening Ritual

Each session should begin with this ritual.

LIGHTING OF THE CANDLES

Ohemma: We light these candles as a symbol of our souls and the symbol of the souls of all women. Who are we?

Group: We are beautiful African-American women, created by a loving God. We are victorious over the forces of oppression that are designed to destroy us. No weapon formed against us shall prosper, for we are more than conquerors through the One who saves us, Jesus Christ, the Anointed One.

POURING THE LIBATION

Ohemma: We pour this water in gratitude to God for the women on whose shoulders we stand. (*Pour some of the water.*) This water is a symbol of the life force of the universe that nourished them and nourishes our souls with new life, health, and strength. (*Pour some more.*) We are being renewed daily by the power of the Holy Spirit in us, and we are born again as daughters of faith, through the saving grace of Jesus Christ. (*Pour again.*) We thank God for the biblical women who have gone before, daughters of faith, who gave us a foundation.

Group: (*Name biblical women such as Deborah, Esther, Phoebe while the Ohemma pours.*)

Ohemma: We thank God for the African-American women who have gone before, daughters of faith, who kept up the struggle.

Group: (*Name women from Black History while the Ohemma pours.*)

Ohemma: We thank God for the women in our families, daughters of faith, who kept the family going.

Group: (*Name female family members while the Ohemma pours.*) Amen!

PRAYER AND PRAISE

(*All hold hands. An Elder leads the group in prayer. Praise and worship may include singing, affirmations, recitation of the Daughters of Imani Code of Conduct, movement, and poetry.*)

Permission is granted to the purchaser to photocopy this page for use with DAUGHTERS OF IMANI: A CHRISTIAN RITES OF PASSAGE FOR AFRICAN-AMERICAN YOUNG WOMEN, © 2005 by Abingdon Press. All rights reserved.

Daughters of Imani
Closing Ritual

Each session should end with this ritual.

DIMMING OF THE CANDLES

Ohemma: These candles are a symbol of our souls and the symbol of the souls of all women. Our souls shine even as the candles are dimmed. (*Snuff the candles.*) We know who we are even as we move out of this circle into our daily lives. Who are we?

Group: We are beautiful African-American women, created by a loving God. We are victorious over the forces of oppression that are designed to destroy us. No weapon formed against us shall prosper, for we are more than conquerors through the One who saves us, Jesus Christ, the Anointed One.

DAUGHTERS OF IMANI CIRCLE CHANT

The girls hold hands, forming a circle

Older women hold hands, forming a circle around the girls.

All hands remain held throughout, except after saying, "Women of God!"

All: Daughters of Imani! (*Hands are down.*)
  Isoke! (*Hands raised up.*)
  Malika! (*Hands are down.*)
  Aisha! (*Hands raised up.*)
  Naima! (*Hands are down.*)
  Ifeoma! (*Hands raised up.*)
  Women of God! (*Hands are released and held up in praise to God; head lifted up in reverence to God.*)

Permission is granted to the purchaser to photocopy this page for use with **DAUGHTERS OF IMANI: A CHRISTIAN RITES OF PASSAGE FOR AFRICAN-AMERICAN YOUNG WOMEN**, © 2005 by Abingdon Press. All rights reserved.

Daughters of Imani Pledge

Let us all stand as we make our pledge:

We will remember the lives, glory, trials,
and tribulations of our ancestors

And honor the struggles of our elders.

We will strive to bring new values and new life to our people;

We will have peace and unity among us.

We will be loving, sharing, and creative.

We will work, study, and listen

So that we may learn and then go out and teach.

We will have discipline, patience, devotion, and courage.

We will live as models to provide new direction for our people.

We will be free and self-determined.

We are Daughters of Imani, journeying toward womanhood.

DAUGHTERS OF IMANI!

Permission is granted to the purchaser to photocopy this page for use with DAUGHTERS OF IMANI: A CHRISTIAN RITES OF PASSAGE FOR AFRICAN-AMERICAN YOUNG WOMEN, © 2005 by Abingdon Press. All rights reserved.

Sisters of Niara Affirmation

I am a Sister of Niara.
I am destined to make a difference.
Why, you may ask?
Well, listen up; and here's the real deal.
First, I love God
With all of my heart, soul, mind, and strength.
Second, I love my neighbor as I love myself.
It is my mission to change the world.
No longer do I listen to the world,
But I get my marching orders from God.
I've checked out this world;
I will not conform,
But I will be transformed by the renewing of my mind.
No longer will I ask what God can do for me,
But I will ask what I can do for God.
In God, I find my true purpose, my higher purpose;
And that is ...
TO CHANGE THE WORLD!

Daughters of Imani Affirmation

We are Daughters of Imani, Sisters in the Spirit,

Children of the Most High,

Spiritual ambassadors

Representing God.

The devil can't stop us,

And you sure can't brush us by.

We are led by

YHWH,

Elohim,

El-Shaddai,

Creator, Provider, Sustainer, Savior,

GOD!

Code of Conduct

Our Code of Conduct governs our behavior as Children of God and members of Daughters of Imani.

We will begin each session by affirming ourselves.

We will always maintain manners and posture worthy of our royal heritage and carry ourselves with pride and dignity.

We will always demonstrate respect for ourselves and for the rights and properties of others.

We will always do our best to help one another achieve our goals and dreams.

We will never say negative or discouraging things to one another.

We will always strive for the highest character, integrity, and honesty and maintain a passion for excellence in what we do.

We will clean up after ourselves.

We will treat the church with the utmost respect.

WE WILL APPLY THESE CODES AND PLEDGES, KNOWING THAT GOD IS ALWAYS WATCHING.

Daughters of Imani
The Call to Celebrate

LEADER: This is the day that the Lord has made!

ALL: **We will rejoice and be glad in it!**

LEADER: This is a day of great celebration! We are gathered together as God's children to honor our elders and celebrate our young people.

ALL: **We celebrate our generational connectedness.**

LEADER: This is a day of great rejoicing! As God's children, we gather in unity to celebrate our love for God and for one another, for we know that where there is unity, there is strength.

ALL: **We celebrate our strength.**

LEADER: This is a day of jubilation! We celebrate those women who serve as role models, mentors, and extraordinary women of faith. We have come to witness our daughters cross over the threshold from childhood into the journey of young adulthood.

ALL: **We celebrate African-American womanhood.**

LEADER: Let us praise God for the great things God has done. Let us praise God for blessing us right now. Let us praise God for a bright tomorrow. Let us celebrate the Father, let us celebrate the Son, and let us celebrate the Holy Spirit.

ALL: **We praise you, O God. We praise our Lord, Jesus Christ. And we praise the Holy Spirit. Now let the celebration begin!**

Permission is granted to the purchaser to photocopy this page for use with DAUGHTERS OF IMANI: A CHRISTIAN RITES OF PASSAGE FOR AFRICAN-AMERICAN YOUNG WOMEN, © 2005 by Abingdon Press. All rights reserved.

Daughters of Imani
Crossing Over Ceremony

(This ceremony marks the initiates' completion of the requirements for graduation from the program. All youth participants are asked to wear white, except for the graduates, who are asked to wear purple. Mentors, elders, and other volunteers should wear purple or black.)

PROCESSIONAL OF OHEMMA, COUNCIL OF ELDERS, AND DAUGHTERS OF IMANI WITH MENTORS

Ohemma: We light these candles as a symbol of our souls and the symbol of the souls of all women. My sisters and my daughters, you are here today to follow in the footsteps of your ancestors and your sisters who have gone before you. You have received the instruction and training necessary to cross over into the journey of young adulthood.

When you were born, you came from your mother's womb into the light. At that time, you could do nothing on your own. Someone had to take care of you. You had to be clothed, sheltered, raised, and instructed in the ways of life. The job was well done, you stand here today as proof. When you were inducted into Daughters of Imani, you knew nothing of becoming a woman. Who are we?

Group: We are beautiful African-American women, created by a loving God. We are victorious over the forces of oppression that are designed to destroy us. No weapon formed against us shall prosper, for we are more than conquerors through the One who saves us, Jesus Christ, the Anointed One.

(All Daughters of Imani meetings enact the pouring of the libation, symbolizing the power of transformation and regeneration of the Holy Spirit, and of cleansing, forgiveness, and renewal. The Ohemma takes a vessel of water and pours it into a plant, which reflects life, nourishment, and community.)

Ohemma: We pour this water as a symbol of the life force of the universe gushing up into the wells of our souls, nourishing us with new life, health, and strength. We are being renewed daily by the power of the Holy Spirit in us, and we are born again as daughters of faith through the saving grace of Christ.

Group: Amen!

Mentor: Mentors, instructors, and role models have embraced you, taught you, nurtured you, and disciplined you as you started the journey toward womanhood. After months of study, prayer, and fellowship, you stand on the threshold of young adulthood.

As you continue this journey into womanhood, it will not be easy. But if you remain confident in knowing that God has a plan for your good, a plan to give you hope, and a future, nothing shall be impossible for you.

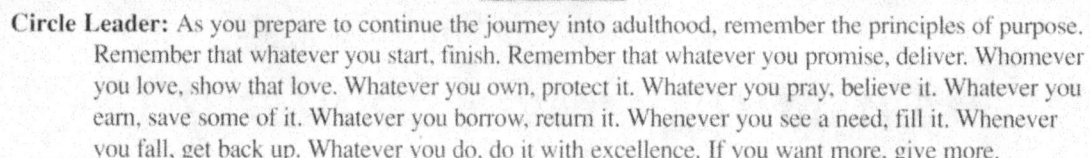

Circle Leader: As you prepare to continue the journey into adulthood, remember the principles of purpose. Remember that whatever you start, finish. Remember that whatever you promise, deliver. Whomever you love, show that love. Whatever you own, protect it. Whatever you pray, believe it. Whatever you earn, save some of it. Whatever you borrow, return it. Whenever you see a need, fill it. Whenever you fall, get back up. Whatever you do, do it with excellence. If you want more, give more.

Circle Leader: God has called you to bring new life to the people of God. Use your gifts and talents to help those who come after you. Now listen to words of inspiration and wisdom shared by your mentor. (*Mentors must be prepared with new names for protegees.*)

Ohemma: The notion of naming has tremendous resonance among African Americans. Black people have been called so many things in this country; and we have responded with continuing efforts to redefine, to counter the negative. All through the process of relationships, the Mentors have gotten to know the girls and have come up with names to describe them. These names reflect their spirit, character, and transformation.

(*Mentors give the protegees new names.*)

Presentation of Honoree

Cultural Presentation and Recitations

Circle Leader: The Book of Proverbs tells us that you should not forsake the law of your mother. Listen now as your mothers share words of wisdom, knowledge, and love.

Parents/Family Elders: Go forward, but understand that womanhood is not just a celebration but the beginning of a new stage of consciousness and responsibility. It is work. It is discipline. It is family. It is community. It is purpose. It is you. Before your community, you enter a larger family. You are a woman, but you are not alone. We challenge you to find your destiny in life, help someone along the way, and leave the world a better place than you found it. Do you commit to this challenge?

(*Ohemma will instruct participants to turn and address the community and use a new name.*)

IT IS I,_____, COMING IN DESIRE OF GOD'S BLESSINGS, MY ANCESTORS' STRENGTH, AND YOUR ADMITTANCE INTO THE YOUNG ADULT COMMUNITY.

Community Response: We admit you.

Ohemma: You have completed the requirements for graduation from Daughters of Imani: A Journey Toward Womanhood Rites of Passage Ministry Class of (*insert year*).

Congratulations, and God bless you.

Benediction
May the grace of God be ever amazing in your life. May goodness and mercy be your constant companions. May you experience the peace of God that the world can't understand. May the blessings of God flow like a never-ending waterfall in your life. Now unto God, who is the Architect of the Universe and the Creator of All, be glory, honor, and praise. Amen.

Permission is granted to the purchaser to photocopy this page for use with **Daughters of Imani: A Christian Rites of Passage for African-American Young Women**, © 2005 by Abingdon Press. All rights reserved.

Daughters of Imani
Mentor Commitment Service

Ohemma: A mentor is a trusted guide and friend who provides care, consistency, candor, communication, and commitment to her protegee. You have come and engaged in the training necessary to serve as a leader and role model of the Daughters of Imani Rites of Passage ministry. Please repeat after me the following pledge of commitment:

With the help of God,

I come desiring to serve,

provide support, guidance, and time

to the Daughters of Imani ministry.

It is my goal to help the daughters

gain skills and confidence

to be responsible for their own future.

With God's help, I will be a positive influence,

always seeking to live a life

worthy of being called a mentor.

PART 2:
The Curriculum

The *Daughters of Imani: A Christian Rites of Passage for African-American Young Women* curriculum piece consists of four units of study: Self-Worth and Self-Esteem, Endurance and Bonding/Family Matters, Health and Sexuality, and Social Grace. The lessons in these units are based on the real-life needs of African-American girls. They all include hands-on activities that provide young people with the opportunity to practice and learn through doing the various skills and topics they will discuss in the small group study sessions. Life application study produces results. Application begins by knowing and understanding the goals of the unit. However, knowing and understanding is not sufficient. Life application methods show the participants how to carry out the focus of the lesson, motivating them to activate their knowledge by putting it into practice in their daily lives.

The small study groups (Sister Circles) are an integral part of the program. Small group study takes place in the Sister Circle meeting. An explanation of the Sister Circle is provided in Chapter 2. These small groups give the participants an intimate opportunity to study and discuss with one another. There is an Elder or a mentor assigned to each Sister Circle to provide leadership, support, and guidance. These groups should meet no fewer than twice a month.

Bible study is crucial to this program. The lessons come in a separate book but are coordinated with the lessons of the program curriculum. Bible study can occur in the small group, the large group, or in a separate session. The Bible study has been placed immediately after the focus in the first three lessons of each unit. However, you may adjust the timing, according to what works best for your group.

Journaling is a skill participants should learn during the course of the program. Each participant will receive a journal in her Survival Kit. The journal is a place where the participant can record her thoughts, prayers, and progress on the journey. To help the girls understand the concept of journaling, give them instructions similar to what follows:

Take your journal, your pen or pencil, and any other necessary items to a quiet and comfortable place. Before you begin journaling, think about the subject matter that you will be writing about. When you have done this, begin your journey in writing. Write as freely as possible, letting your words flow from the pen to the page. Do not worry about spelling or punctuation; just go with the flow. Your journal is the place where you can record your innermost thoughts and feelings. It belongs to you only. You may be asked to share your thoughts with others. However, it is not a requirement. If you would like to share, do so. If you would rather not share, you do not have to.

The role of the *griot* (GREE-oh) is also an important part of the program. *Griot* is a French word that describes the role of historian/storyteller in Senegal, a French-speaking African country. Throughout West Africa, the griot is charged with knowing the history, family lines, and cultural values of the community. During special ceremonies they colorfully relate to the people facts, poetry, songs, and stories concerning the values and history of the people.

Griot Time occurs in most lessons, usually a ten-minute period in which a mentor or elder shares a personal story based on the given subject. This is a time of sharing and testimony, not preaching or sermonizing. It is about sharing a life lesson based on real experience. Sometimes this sharing occurs while the group is working on the community quilt or some other large group project. Persons who serve as griots must be aware of the focus for the day. They must understand that while Griot Time is an opportunity for sharing a part of their life story, the purpose of their testimony is for the benefit of the growth of the young women in their charge.

Portfolio Activity

Dear Daughter,

This portfolio was developed so that you can put some of the lessons that we have discussed into action. Most of this information will require that you remember the discussions that we've had, while some of the information is new. I know that this exercise won't be too hard for you. The portfolio activity encourages you to express your creativity and imagination to really get your point across. Keep all of your portfolio assignments in a folder to keep them organized. Your task is to complete at least one activity each month; however, you may do more if you desire.

1. List all 66 books in the Bible. The list should be in order, and spelling has to be correct. What is your favorite Scripture? Why?

2. List five Bible verses that you like or that you recite often when you become angry so that you can remain calm. If you don't know five, ask a family member, mentor, spiritual leader, or friend to share their favorites with you.

3. List five gospel, praise, worship, or inspirational songs that you enjoy singing. Draw a picture that represents for you the message in each song.

4. Life Lesson: In our culture, we have a saying that "the glass is either half empty or half full." In a two paragraph essay, explain what this saying means and why your glass is half full.

5. Sisters in the Spirit: Sometimes mentors don't know that they are having an impact on your life. Please express to them in writing two examples that show how Daughters of Imani has helped you in specific situations. Also, list three ways that Daughters of Imani can be improved in the future. Finally, list two activities that you will do as a mentor with a group of children when you get older.

6. Knowing Me: Imagine that you have a penpal in another country. What would you like for him or her to know about you? Develop a collage with pictures and other craft items that describe you. Some items that you might show are your likes, dislikes, proudest and saddest moments, family, school, teachers, friends, and so forth.

7. Career Planning: Write a 50- to 100-word essay on your future plans, such as college, graduate school, career, family, lifestyle, where you will live. After writing your essay, create a goals sheet that includes short-term, midterm, and long-range goals for achieving your career plans.

8. History of Our People: The month of February is Black History Month, and March is Women's History Month. Pick three African-American women, and describe their accomplishments and how their accomplishments affect you.

9. Budgeting: Develop a list of your top seven wants and top seven needs. From that list, put them in order of priority to determine your top three wants and top three needs for living.

From Rev. Richelle

Curriculum Overview

Unit 1: Self-Worth and Self-Esteem

Learning Goals
- Learn how culture and personal relationships affect feelings of self-worth.
- Understand that a relationship with Jesus Christ can have a positive effect on feelings of self-worth.
- Have the opportunity to honestly appraise feelings of self-worth and reflect on ways of deepening and increasing that self-worth.

Bible Study
John 4:1-39 (the woman at the well)
1 Kings 10:1-13 (the Queen of Sheba)

Session	Session Title	Session Goals
1	Self-Image and the Media (Hip-Hop Culture)	Participants will take an honest look at themselves and their culture.
2	Declaration of Self-Esteem	Participants will declare how God gives them self-worth.
3	Developing Healthy Self-Esteem	Participants will examine their own likes, dislikes, and values.
4	Relationship With Christ and Others	Participants will draw upon their relationship with Christ to grow in leadership skills.

Unit 2: Endurance and Bonding/Family Matters

Learning Goals
- Examine personal family structure.
- Develop and appreciation for their families and relationships.
- Practice spiritual ways of communicating in relationship.

Bible Study
Numbers 27 (the daughters of Zelophehad)
Ruth 1–4 (Naomi and Ruth)

Session	Session Title	Session Goals
1	My Family, Me, and You	Participants will examine ways of being family: Who belongs and how?
2	Understanding My Family	Participants will think about family needs and issues.
3	Praying for One Another	Participants will develop prayer partnerships.
4	Heritage	Participants will be introduced to African and African-American history.

Unit 3: Health and Sexuality

Learning Goals
- Have the opportunity to confront personal views on sexuality and the body.
- Learn positive methods of caring for the body.
- Gain access to information concerning health and sexuality of Black woman.

Bible Study
Mark 5:25-34 (the woman with an issue of blood)
Judges 4:1-10 (the story of Deborah)

Session	Session Title	Session Goals
1	Healthful Living for African-American Girls	Participants will learn more about healthy living and lifestyles.
2	Responsible Sexuality and Celibacy	Participants will have the opportunity to discuss sexuality, life, culture, with mentors.
3	Sexually Transmitted Diseases and HIV/AIDS	Participants will gain information about STDs and pregnancy.
4	HIV/AIDS: The Truth Shall Set You Free	Participants will learn to distinguish between fact and fiction concerning AIDS.

Unit 4: Social Grace

Learning Goals
- Evaluate styles of dress, clothing, and their contexts.
- Learn deportment and manners appropriate for various settings.
- Think about career choices.

Bible Study
Esther
Romans 16:1-2 (Phoebe)

Session	Session Title	Session Goals
1	Character in Social Life and Relationships	Participants will think about social life, reputation, and relationship among women.
2	Table Hospitality	Participants will have the opportunity to be graceful while eating in community.
3	Beauty and Bounty	Participants will deal with outward appearance and becoming a women of substance.
4	Time and Money Management	Participants will discuss a management plan that promotes physical, mental/emotional, financial, social, and spiritual well-being.

Unit 1

Self-Worth and Self-Esteem

This broad area covers the development of positive self-esteem and positive self-concept within each participant. These lessons will guide leaders and participants through practical means of building positive self-worth as a method to becoming leaders in the African-American community and the world at large.

African-American women often struggle for positive recognition and imaging in American society. The struggle continues even as history is full of the success stories of self-affirming Black women who defy the odds and do extraordinary things. Social, cultural, political, and even religious structures often combine to create a fairly negative perception of Black women. Therefore, the necessity for encouraging and developing self-worth in African-American girls and women is one that must be continually addressed.

Self-worth consists of self-esteem and self-image. Self-esteem is how a girl feels about herself. Self-image is how a girl thinks the rest of the world sees her. Both of these form her overall self-worth. By honestly appraising her self-esteem and her self-image, a girl can make a conscious assessment of how she feels about herself. In so doing, each girl may then begin working on strategies that positively improve her self-esteem. By lifting up strong faith and spirituality for young girls to grab hold of, as well as positive images, role models, and tactics for developing healthy self-esteem, it is possible for girls to overcome the negative influences in our culture. Mentoring relationships are ideal for nurturing the kinds of needs that young girls have in striving to construct spiritual ways of being that will enable them to withstand the racism, sexism, and consumerism of modern society.

UNIT LEARNING GOALS
- Learn how culture and personal relationships affect feelings of self-worth.
- Understand that a relationship with Jesus Christ can have a positive effect on feelings of self-worth.
- Have the opportunity to honestly appraise feelings of self-worth and reflect on ways of deepening and increasing that self-worth.

Bible study for this unit may be John 4:1-39 (the woman at the well) and/or 1 Kings 10:1-13 (the Queen of Sheba).

1
Self-Image and the Media
(Hip Hop Culture)

Sister Souljah is a contemporary leader who is vocal about the negative images of African-American women in the media and the harmful effects of racism on the psychology of young people. Suggestions for the presentation include: 1) reading aloud excerpts from her autobiography, *No Disrespect** (page *x* (in the introduction), paragraph 1, and pages 34–35, beginning with "Of course, like any child..." and ending with "...follow me forever"); 2) putting on a dramatic skit or a reader's theater, presenting her views for empowerment and self-esteem in the African-American community.

> * *No Disrespect* contains graphic information concerning the difficulties of growing up poor, Black, and female in certain troubled urban communities of New York City. There are references to sexual and drug activity. While much of this autobiography may not represent appropriate reading for young girls, this writing is a testimony to the strength of the human spirit as grounded in faith in God. The recommended excerpts indicate that self-worth and spiritual strength are necessary for the struggle.

LESSON FOCUS
In this lesson, participants will take an honest look at themselves and their culture. The fact is that the dominant cultural trend for American young people, especially Blacks, is hip-hop in all of its various forms: music, videos, clothes, language, style, attitude, and mentality. Even young people being raised in the most protective environments are aware of hip-hop and its influence. This session will help the participants begin to explore this culture and the impact that it has on their lives, consciously and subconsciously.

The American media, through movies, television, commercials, print and video advertisements, music, and videos, often contains images that are harmful to African-American girls and women. Sexual activity, violence, and drug life are glorified; and the presentation of African-American women, particularly in hip-hop videos, can be quite demeaning. Women in these videos are displayed in sexually suggestive and degrading ways: as physical objects of desire and control. These images promote an assumption that the value of women of color comes only from their physical appearance, and their relation to the opposite sex is a commodity to be controlled. Moreover, images of brutality and violence toward young women create the perception that women of color are rightfully physically exploited and abused. Studies are beginning to indicate a direct correlation between the images of women in hip-hop culture and negative social effects.

Opening Ritual With Prayer and Praise (page 46)

Celebration of Women (page 5)

BIBLE STUDY

SISTER CIRCLES
Activity 1: A Demonstration Skit
For this skit, you will need the following:
Δ one participant who stands
Δ one participant who cuts an oversized T-shirt
Δ one Elder who verbally leads the presentation and explains the effects of negativity on self-esteem
Δ one old, oversized T-shirt
Δ one regular sized T-shirt
Δ craft items: scissors, fabric paints, paint brushes, iron-ons

Select a participant who will stand in front of the group wearing both T-shirts. Let her put on a regular sized T-shirt and then put oversized T-shirt over the regular one. The oversized T-shirt is to be cut with scissors in order to make a point of how negativity damages self-esteem.

As the first volunteer stands in front of the group, have the other participants name some of negative comments they have heard people say to others. For every negative comment, the second volunteer will make a cut in the outer T-shirt. Then ask the group to repeat negative comments they have heard in their own household. Again, the second volunteer makes the cuts with the scissors. When finished, the Elder slowly spins the first volunteer around and explains how every negative comment affects a person's sense of self-worth. It is said that every negative stroke a person receives from others require seven positive strokes to patch up the damage to the self. A person's self-worth is constructed by how she believes others on the outside perceive her (self-image) and how she feels about herself on the inside (self-esteem).

Discuss the following questions about the Demonstration Skit:
1. Did the demonstration help you understand the impact of negativity on self-esteem and self-perception?
2. What are some of the negative things that you think cause low self-esteem?
3. Are there things in your life that may cause you to feel like you have low self-esteem? What are they?
4. How can one develop and keep a strong self-esteem?
5. Discuss building a strong self-image based on your inner perception of yourself so that you cannot be negatively affected by other people's outside perception.

Activity 2: Creating Positive Rap
For this activity, you will need the following:
△ *This Is Your Life* CD, by Out of Eden
△ CD player
△ regular sized T-shirt for each participant

Have the group listen to "Showpiece," from the CD. Out of Eden is a contemporary gospel/hip-hop group, consisting of three African-American sisters: Lisa Kimmey Bragg (producer), Andrea Kimmey Baca, Joy Danielle Kimmey. They have been in the Christian music business for ten years, being nominated for a Dove Award in 1994 for their debut album *Lovin' the Day*. In 2003, their album *This Is Your Life* won four Dove Awards; while Lisa won three more as producer. These young women want to "set a standard as a truly positive voice." Their dependence on God, their confidence in their abilities, and their willingness to commit to hard work is indicative of women who have positive self-worth in Jesus Christ.

Discuss the words to "Showpiece":
1. What words show that the girl feels as though someone is trying to control her?
2. What is a "showpiece"? How is this term used to describe some women?
3. In popular culture, what imagery and ideology are used against Black women?
4. What phrases indicate the singer's sense of positive self-worth?

This conversation may occur while participants are decorating their own T-shirts. The T-shirt creations should lift up the positive in their own personalities and ways of being. Pieces of these shirts can be used for the community quilt. Or you may choose to have the participants create an upbeat contemporary rap/song based on positive comment about each other.

GRIOT TIME
One Elder or Mentor should take no more than 10 minutes to tell about a time when she felt badly about being Black and female. She must be sure to include how she began to feel better about it.

CLOSING
After allowing time for participants to write in their journals, do the Closing Ritual.

Closing Ritual (page 47)

Opening Ritual With Prayer and Praise (page 46)

Celebration of Women (page 17)

2
Declaration of Self-Esteem

Nana Yaa Asantewa (YAH ah-SAHN-teh-WAH) was a great Ashanti queen mother and warrior, one of the most revered women in Ashanti history because of her love for her people. *Ashanti* has become a popular name for African-American girls and may reflect a pride in the history and culture of the Ashanti people.

Create a visual and auditory background for this presentation by displaying African fabrics, especially kente (an Ashanti design and weave), and by playing African music.

LESSON FOCUS
"Let the redeemed of the LORD say so," instructs Psalm 107:2. The goal of this lesson is to give participants a tool by which they can "say so" and declare how God gives them self-worth. The Declaration of Self-Esteem is an activity that seeks to build positive self-esteem within each participant. This activity will also acquaint participants with adinkra symbols. The adinkra symbols are part of the Akan culture of Ghana in West Africa. Originally, the symbols memorialized loved ones. The grieving families stamped onto their clothing the symbols that represented personality characteristics. Through studying the positive affirmations found in these symbols, participants will develop a tool that boosts self-esteem.

BIBLE STUDY

SISTER CIRCLES
Activity 1: Adinkra Declarations of Self-Esteem
For this activity, you will need the following:
Δ photocopies of the Adinkra Symbols handout (page 68) (You may wish to supplement the handout by creating an additional handout of adinkra symbols and their meanings for inclusion in the girls' scrapbooks or portfolios. Adinkra symbols can be readily found in library books and on the Internet on sites such as *www.welltempered.net/adinkra/htmls/adinkra_index.htm.*)
Δ photocopies of the Self-Esteem Scriptures handout (page 69) for each participant
Δ basic formation about Ghana (found on the Internet)
Δ 11-by-14 fadeless construction paper (assorted colors)
Δ 8½-by-11 white paper
Δ chart paper

Δ large, unlined index cards
Δ writing and drawing implements: color pencils, markers, pens, pencils
Δ assorted magazines that may be cut up
Δ rulers

Ask the participants to define the word *declaration*. Ask them to write their responses on chart paper. Tell them that a *declaration* is a "statement that a person says with inspiration and conviction." Ask them to define *self-esteem* and to write their responses on the chart paper. Tell them that *self-esteem* is a "person's opinion of himself or herself." A person may have either positive or negative self-esteem. Our goal for today is to build our self-esteem by declaring to the world (saying with inspiration and conviction) who we are. Before proceeding, answer any questions that may arise.

Distribute to each girl the information about adinkra symbols. Tell about historical and contemporary uses of adinkra symbols. Then hand out some basic formation about Ghana. Ghana is formerly known as the Gold Coast and is the home of the Ashanti, the Akan, and the Twi people.

Have the students look over the adinkra symbols and talk about the ones that appeal to them. Read over the definitions for the symbols with the students, have them talk about which symbols describe or speak to who they are as a person.

Ask the participants to choose seven symbols as the foundation for their project. Participants should write the name of the symbol and its meaning in their journals or portfolios.

Distribute the Self-Esteem Scriptures handouts. Give the participants a few moments to read over the Scriptures. Ask them to talk about the Scriptures that help them better understand who God is and who God created them to be.

Now ask the participants to choose one of their symbols and choose a Bible verse that corresponds with the definition. Say, for example, "This symbol (point to the symbol), *fihankra* (fee-HAHN-krah), represents security and safety. It might be paired with the Scripture: 'God is our refuge and strength, a very present help in trouble' (Psalm 46:1)." Participants may write the verse as it is, or they may rewrite the words to make it more personal. An example for the same Scripture passage might be: "God is my strength and security. I am safe with God even when there is trouble." However, participants do not have to match Scriptures and symbols. They may simply choose Scriptures that speak to their self-esteem, and write them as affirmations.

An example of an adinkra symbol that symbolizes "God's presence and power are always with me" is *nyame nnwu na mawu* (in-YAH-may in-IN-woo NAH MAH-woo), which means, "God never dies, therefore I cannot die." The Scripture match might be: "For I am convinced that neither death, nor life, nor angels nor rulers, nor things present, nor things to come, nor powers, nor height, nor depth, nor anything else in all creation, will be able to separate us from the love of God in Christ Jesus our Lord" (Romans 8:38-39).

Another example might be derived from two symbols, representing "I am a child of God. How can I lose?" The symbols *nyame biribi wo soro* (in-YAH-may bee-REE-bee WOH SOH-roh), meaning "God is in the heavens," and *nsoromma* (in-SOH-ROH-mah), meaning "Child of the heavens," can be paired with the Scripture: "If God is for us, who is against us?" (Romans 8:31b).

After choosing the symbols, writing their definitions, and identifying Scripture passages, each participant will begin to create her declaration of self-esteem. To create a declaration, the participants will write a sentence of affirmation about each symbol that she has chosen. Each sentence should contain one of these words: *God, the Lord, Jesus,* and either *me* or *I*. This helps the participants realize that only God and self can define who we are.

Encourage the participants to use a combination of self-created and Bible-inspired affirmations. Participants may choose to rearrange or rewrite the words of a verse in order to personalize it. Participants should write their declaration in their journals or portfolios. Allow the opportunity for those who wish to share to do so. After the girls have completed their declarations, have them proofread one another's work for spelling and grammar. Then have the participants use markers, pens, or color pencils to write their declarations on a large index card.

Activity 2: Say It With Self-Esteem
For this activity, you will need the following:
Δ index cards
Δ markers
Δ bookmarks for prizes

Create two sets of Say It With Self-Esteem cue cards by writing the following affirmations (including the numbers) on index cards (one affirmation on each card for each set):

1. Attitude is a little thing that makes a big difference.
2. There is greatness inside of me.
3. God made me special.
4. My attitude determines my altitude.
5. Where there is knowledge there is power.
6. My world is as big as I make it.
7. God is the same yesterday, today, and forevermore.
8. I can do all things through Christ, who strengthens me.
9. I am more than a conqueror in Christ Jesus.
10. I can and will make a difference.

Divide the group into two teams, and have each team choose a team captain. Give each team captain a set of the cue cards. The captain will then hand out the cards to team members, including herself. The captain may hand out the cards at random; or she may choose to hand them out according to the affirmation on the card, matching particular affirmations with particular teammates.

If there are more cards than team members, the team captain should hand out the extras to whichever teammates she chooses. **If there are fewer cards than team members,** the team captain will line up the girls without cards behind those who have cards. After a team member has said her affirmation, she hands her card to the first teammate without a card.

After the cards are distributed, ask the girls to line up, single file, according to the number on their card. (For those who have more than one card, ask them to line up according to the lowest number in their hand.)

Explain that the cards contain affirmations that must be said in a positive manner. Participants will compete against a player on the opposite team. The objective is for the player to say the affirmation with more conviction and passion than her opponent. The Elder decides which team starts first.

To begin the game, have two opponents with a number 1 cue card stand before the judges, Mentors or other adult volunteers. One at a time, the two opponents say their affirmation with as much conviction and passion as they can muster. The participant who wins the round, according to the judges, will be awarded a point for her team.

The game continues until all of the affirmations have been said. Award the winning team with bookmarks that have an affirmation on them.

Variation: Have the participants rap or sing the affirmation.

GRIOT TIME
An Elder or Mentor should take no more than 10 minutes to talk about a time when she felt absolutely great about being Black and female.

CLOSING
After allowing time for participants to write in their journals, do the Closing Ritual.

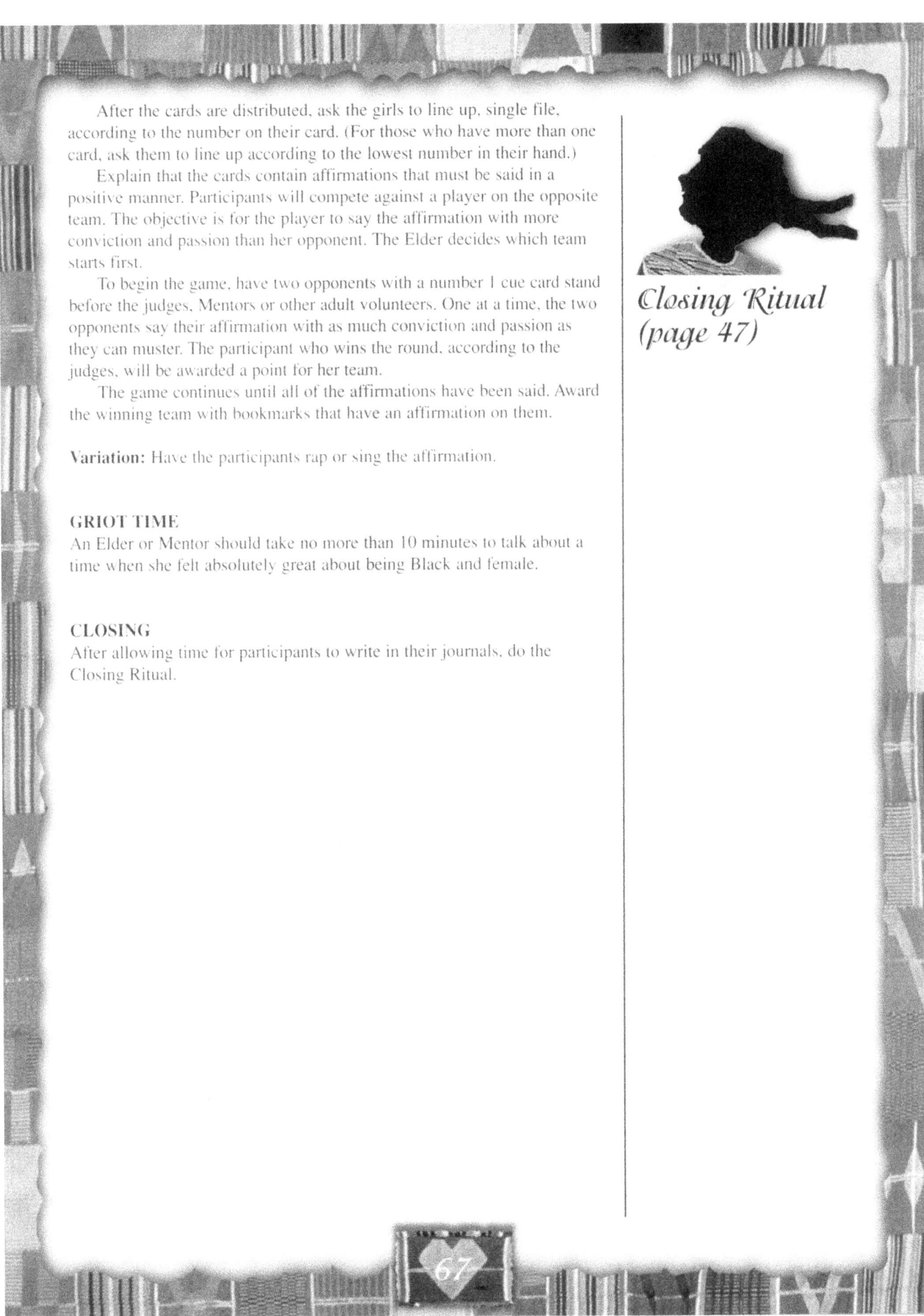

Closing Ritual (page 47)

Adinkra Symbols

Use these adinkra symbols (and any others you may find) along with the Self-Esteem Scriptures (page 69) to help you to better understand who God is and who God created you to be.

Adinkrahene
(ah-DEEN-krah-HEE-nay)

Symbolizes: greatness, charisma, leadership

Nsoromma
(in-SOH-ROH-mah)

Symbolizes: guardianship

Akoma
(ah-KOH-mah)

Symbolizes: patience, tolerance

Nyame Biribi Wo Soro
(in-YAH-may bee-REE-bee WOH SOH-roh)

Symbolizes: hope

Fihankra
(fee-HAHN-krah)

Symbolizes: security, safety

Nya Nnwu Na Mawu
(in-YAH in-NOO-woo NAH MAH-woo)

Symbolizes: life after death

Mate Masie
(MAH-tay MAH-see-AY)

Symbolizes: wisdom, knowledge, prudence

Nyansapo
(in-YAHN-SAH-poh)

Symbolizes: wisdom, ingenuity, intelligence, patience

Permission is granted to the purchaser to photocopy this page for use with DAUGHTERS OF IMANI: A CHRISTIAN RITES OF PASSAGE FOR AFRICAN-AMERICAN YOUNG WOMEN, © 2005 by Abingdon Press. All rights reserved.

Self-Esteem Scriptures

Use these Scriptures, along with adinkra symbols (see page 68), to help you to better understand who God is and who God created you to be.

Jeremiah 29:11	Surely I know the plans I have for you, says the LORD, plans for your welfare and not for harm, to give you a future with hope.
Proverbs 3:26	The LORD will be your confidence.
Philippians 4:13	I can do all things through him who strengthens me.
Matthew 10:16b	Be as wise as serpents and innocent as doves.
Romans 8:31b	If God is for us, who is against us?
Romans 8:37	In all these things we are more than conquerors through him who loved us.
Romans 8:38-39	I am convinced that neither death, nor life, nor angels nor rulers, nor things present, nor things to come, nor powers, nor height, nor depth, nor anything else in all creation, will be able to separate us from the love of God in Christ Jesus our Lord.
1 John 5:5	Who is it that conquers the world but the one who believes that Jesus is the Son of God.
1 Peter 2:9	You are a chosen race, a royal priesthood, a holy nation, God's own people.
2 Peter 3:18	Grow in the grace and knowledge of our Lord and Savior Jesus Christ.
Psalm 46:1	God is our refuge and strength, a very present help in trouble.
Psalm 29:11	May the LORD give strength to his people!
Psalm 34:14	Depart from evil and do good; seek peace, and pursue it.
Psalm 27:1	The LORD is my light and my salvation; whom shall I fear? The LORD is the stronghold of my life; of whom shall I be afraid?
Psalm 103:1	Bless the LORD, O my soul, and all that is within me, bless his holy name.
Genesis 1:27	God created humankind in his image, in the image of God he created them; male and female he created them.
Job 23:10	I shall come out like gold.
Proverbs 31:30	A woman who fears the LORD is to be praised.
Psalm 139:14	I praise you, for I am fearfully and wonderfully made.

Permission is granted to the purchaser to photocopy this page for use with DAUGHTERS OF IMANI: A CHRISTIAN RITES OF PASSAGE FOR AFRICAN-AMERICAN YOUNG WOMEN, © 2005 by Abingdon Press. All rights reserved.

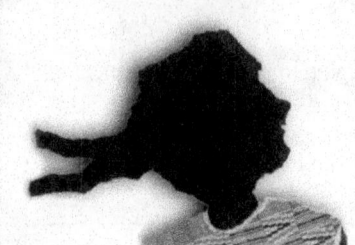

Opening Ritual With Prayer and Praise (page 46)

Celebration of Women (page 9)

3
Developing Healthy Self-Esteem

Maya Angelou is known for her beautiful poetry and prose that examines society from the lens of an African-American woman. Her verses are affirming and positive for Black women, and inspirational in the areas of personal development and self-worth. Introduce this segment by reading the essay "Voices of Respect," from *Wouldn't Take Nothing for My Journey Now*.

LESSON FOCUS
What is self-esteem? *Self-esteem* is defined by the American Heritage Dictionary as "pride in oneself; self-respect." In a world where women still struggle for political, economic, and social equity, attaining positive self-esteem is an issue. The 2003 movie *Real Women Have Curves* shows how body image is part of the picture for all women. Additionally, African-American girls have much more to consider in that the traditional image of the American female beauty remains White and blonde. Therefore, simply by existing in this society, African-American girls, their families, and communities must make a conscious effort to lift up positive images and role models for young Black women to counteract their marginalized role in mainstream culture.

In this session, participants have the opportunity to look inward, examining their own likes, dislikes, and values. They will also examine relationships that have positively affected their growing-up process. They will use body movement and creativity to joyfully relate to one another. Relationships have a tremendous impact on the progress and self-esteem of girls. When those relationships consist of girls and women, especially with women transmitting positive and substantive values onto the developing girls, the result is higher self-esteem.

BIBLE STUDY

SISTER CIRCLES
Activity 1: Part 1—All About Me
For this activity, you will need the following:
Δ photocopies of the All About Me activity sheet (page 72)
Δ pens or pencils

Give each participant the All About Me activity sheet. Have the youth fill out the sheets. They may individualize their lists by adding information of their own choosing for numbers 9 and 10.

On the back side of the sheet, participants should write, "I am," ten times down left edge of the page. They will add a word or two behind each "I am" statement.

Encourage the participants to be creative and to think of all of the words they can to describe themselves. For example: "I am Black." "I am beautiful." "I am tall." After the first four or five words, the youth may have difficulty thinking of personal characteristics to list.

Have the girls present their two lists to their small groups, developing skits, monologues, raps, or songs to tell about their qualities and the things they like to do. Girls may work in groups or alone, but the object is for them to showcase their talents and also help age-level small groups get to know one another.

Activity 1: Part 2—What Do I Value?
For this activity, you will need the following:
Δ photocopies of What Do I Value? activity sheets (page 72)
Δ pens or pencils

Hand out the What Do I Value? activity sheets for the young women to complete. Have them work in small groups with their mentors to complete the activity sheets and discuss the results.

Activity 2: "Phenomenal Woman"
For this activity, you will need the following:
Δ photocopies of the poem "Phenomenal Woman," by Maya Angelou. This poem can be found in collections, including *Maya Angelou: Poems*, by Maya Angelou, and *Still I Rise*, by Maya Angelou (see page 127 for more information). It may also be found on sites on the Internet. Circle Leaders may choose the following suggestions for younger age-levels: "Little Soul Sister," by Useni Eugene Perkins; "My People," by Langston Hughes; "Who Can Be Born Black," by Mari Evans; and "Your World," by Georgia Douglas Johnson, can all be found in *Make a Joyful Sound: Poems for Children by African-American Poets* (see page 127).

Divide the participants into four groups, one for each stanza of the poem. They may take turns reading, pantomiming, dancing to it, and/or acting it out. Let them come up with a presentation with which all of the members of each small group are satisfied. Small groups will come together for the last few minutes and the entire group will present the whole poem. Note that the last three lines of each stanza are the same. Participants may choose to have a unifying movement for these lines.

GRIOT TIME
One Elder or Mentor should take no more than 10 minutes to talk about a woman other than her own primary caretaker who made a difference in her life. (Increasingly in society, the primary caretaker is not the biological mother.) Before sharing, the griot may read from the essay "Annual Conventions of Everyday Subjects," from *Racism 101*, by Nikki Giovanni (page 84, from "As the poet began..." to "...wasn't tall.")

CLOSING
After allowing time for participants to write in their journals, do the Closing Ritual.

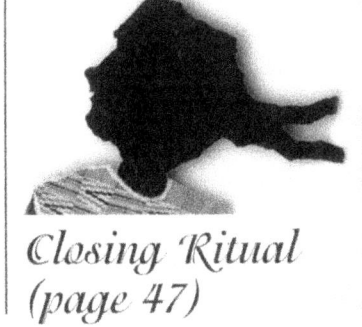

Closing Ritual (page 47)

All About Me

1. My Ethnic Heritage _____
   _____

2. My Favorite Food _____
   _____

3. My Best Time of Day _____
   _____

4. My Age _____
   _____

5. My Favorite Game _____
   _____

6. My Hero _____
   _____

7. My Hobby _____
   _____

8. Title of a Book About Me _____
   _____

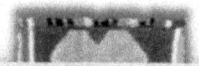

Permission is granted to the purchaser to photocopy this page for use with **DAUGHTERS OF IMANI: A CHRISTIAN RITES OF PASSAGE FOR AFRICAN-AMERICAN YOUNG WOMEN**, © 2005 by Abingdon Press. All rights reserved.

What Do I Value?

Rank in order the following values, from the most important (1) to the least important (12) to you.

_____ honesty

_____ financial security

_____ an exciting life

_____ concern for others

_____ health

_____ religion

_____ self-respect

_____ loyal friendship

_____ education

_____ family

_____ other _____

_____ other _____

My top three values on this list are _____.

My lowest value on this is _____.

Something I learned about myself is _____.

4
Relationships With Christ and Others

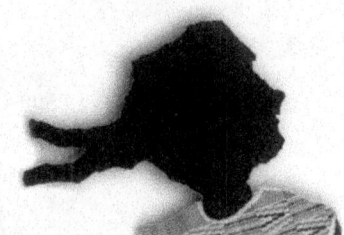

Opening Ritual With Prayer and Praise (page 46)

Celebration of Women (page 13)

(The format is of this session slightly different from the others. Also, by this session, participants should have had the appropriate Bible studies.)

OPENING

The Ohemma and Elders will conduct a guided meditation. This meditation is designed to help the girls relax, go inside themselves, and feel the power of the Holy Spirit. It should last no less than ten minutes and serve as an example so that girls can practice meditation on their own and with others.

After the Opening Ritual and Libation, play soft music or use a trickling water fountain. Ask the entire group to sit in a large circle in chairs or on the floor. Encourage the participants to be as comfortable as possible, to close their eyes, and to breathe deeply. Do not begin the guided statements until each girl is completely quiet and breathing. Pause ten counts between each statement.

Ohemma: In the name of Jesus, we call on your presence Holy Spirit, to dwell with us. *(Pause 10 counts.)*

We call on your presence, O Lord. Come and fill us with your Holy Spirit. *(Pause.)*

Lift us up in your love. *(Pause.)*

Help us feel you as we still our minds, open our hearts, and offer up our souls to you completely, as daughters of faith. *(Pause.)*

Elder: In your Word, Jesus, you say, "The water that I will give will become in them a spring of water gushing up to eternal life." *(Pause.)*

Give us this eternal water, Jesus. Let us go the well that never runs dry. *(Pause.)*

Refresh us; cleanse us; wash us; nurture us; quench our thirst. *(Pause.)*

Ohemma: In this silence, O Jesus, Lamb of God, we invoke your Holy Spirit of Eternal Water to pour the Living Spirit into the wells of our souls. *(Stay silent for 5 minutes.)*

Let us pray softly the Lord's Prayer together. As we pray, alternate your breathing on each line. For example, "Our Father," *(breathe in)* "who art in heaven" *(breathe out)*, and so forth. After the Lord's Prayer, we will silently lift up petitions to God in our hearts.

(Pray, then be silent.) Amen.

Group: Amen!

The presentation on Sojourner Truth may include performing excerpts from *The Narrative of Sojourner Truth*, such as one of her most famous speeches, "Ain't I a Woman?" Excerpts from this speech and others can be found on page 186 of *Crossing the Danger Water: Three Hundred Years of African-American Writing*, edited by Deirdre Mullane; and on pages 524–527 of *Epic Lives: One Hundred Black Women Who Made a Difference*, edited by Jessie Carney Smith. The Elders and girls are encouraged to be creative in developing these presentations.

LESSON FOCUS

In this session, participants will draw upon their relationship with Christ to continue to grow in leadership skills. The Samaritan woman was an unlikely leader. However, her personal encounter with Jesus throws her into a leadership role. Participants may experience the living Christ in a different way during the guided meditation. They, like the Samaritan woman, will be encouraged to look at Christ as the one who helps them to feel good about themselves. The Samaritan woman was empowered by her personal relationship with Christ to go out and share with others the amazing love of God. In contrast, the Queen of Sheba was the leader of an entire empire that spanned parts of Asia and Africa. A relationship with Jesus Christ may help Daughters of Imani feel empowered, assuming leadership in the community, as did Sojourner Truth. Through the Holy Spirit, God gives persons the gifts the community needs to carry out its purpose. A spiritual gift is a special talent or ability that God gives us. Spiritual gifts, especially in the area of assertiveness and leadership, help us carry out God's purposes. Participants are encouraged to be assertive, reaching out to their friends, family, and associates, and looking forward to becoming the movers and shakers in the church and in the world.

SISTER CIRCLES

Activity 1: Got Gifts? Spiritual Gifts and Leadership (Part 1)
For this activity, you will need the following:

Δ Review the "Youth Questionnaire on Spiritual Gifts," on pages 261–267 in *Discover Your God-Given Gifts*, by Don & Katie Fortune, to create a one-page questionnaire for your participants.
Δ Bibles
Δ newsprint or dry-erase board
Δ markers in many colors

Read the listed Scripture passages and record on the board or newsprint the spiritual gifts, as found in the text—Romans 12:4-8; 1 Corinthians 12:4-30; Ephesians 4:7-12; 1 Peter 4:9-11. Use different color markers for each gift the group identifies. Help participants define the meanings and uses of these various gifts. The Spiritual Gifts Definitions (at right) may help, but you may also want to check with a denominational resource.

Now ask, "Why have we been given spiritual gifts?" Then summarize 1 Peter 4:10 and Ephesians 4:12.

Hand out the one-page questionnaire that you have prepared. Allow no more than 15–20 minutes for girls to complete it.

SPIRITUAL GIFTS DEFINITIONS

Prophecy—the gift to proclaim and speak about the will of God

Service—the gift of doing practical things in order to be of service to others

Teaching—the gift of researching, explaining, and/or giving instruction about the Bible

Exhortation—the gift of encouraging others to live a victorious life

Giving—the gift of generosity

Administration—the gift of organization

Compassion/Mercy—the gift of love

Activity 1: Got Gifts? Spiritual Gifts and Leadership (Part 2)
Using the following assertiveness and leadership discussion questions, engage participants in a discussion on leadership and assertiveness:

1. What is your definition of *leadership*?
2. Choose a female whom you believe demonstrates the gift of leadership. How does she demonstrate leadership?
3. Define the term *assertiveness*. Why is this character trait necessary to be a leader?
4. What places of leadership do you see yourself occupying in the future? How do you plan to make a difference in the world through your leadership skills?
5. It has been said that the Black community is absent of high-quality leadership. Do you agree with this statement? What type of leadership is needed for the Black community to move forward to become a great people?
6. Are Christians called to make a difference? How? What difference do you desire to make?
7. It has been said that to be a leader, one must learn to be a follower. Do you agree with this statement? Why, or why not? Please be prepared to defend your position with your group members.
8. As a leader, list some practical ways that you can use your spiritual gifts?

Activity 2: Community Quilt
For this activity, you will need the following:
Δ fabric given to each participant by her Mentor, an Elder, or a family member
Δ other quilting supplies, such as needles, thread, and scissors

While sitting in a circle, each young woman should tell about her piece of fabric in terms of the person who gave it to her. She should tell a story about how that person affected her community, whether by heading a household, participating in a parent/teacher organization, teaching Sunday school, helping with a Girl Scout troop, serving in a civil office, and so forth. After talking, work on the quilt may continue.

GRIOT TIME
One Elder or Mentor should take no more than 10 minutes to talk about the positive and negative experiences during the first time she had a leadership role.

CLOSING
After allowing time for participants to write in their journals, do the Closing Ritual.

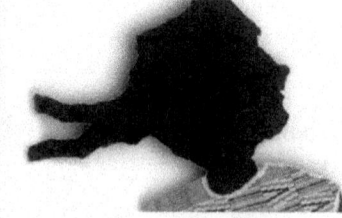

*Closing Ritual
(page 47)*

Unit 2
Endurance and Bonding/ Family Matters

This broad area will encourage bonding among the Daughters, Mentors, and Instructors. It will help participants become more aware of family history, heritage, and dynamics. It will also assist in the development of resiliency skills as well as provide activities for Daughters of Imani to bond with one another.

What is the Black family? What is its influence on the lives of Black girls? The Black family and extended Black family networks have had a direct impact on the development of our communities. The way Black people do family and the family's ability to survive has African roots. However, the Black family, from slavery onward, has been negatively affected by governmental policy and American social structures. Despite structural oppression, negative cultural and social myths, and economic disenfranchisement, the Black family has managed to survive. There is great success in the Black family. However, Black families have been adversely affected emotionally and psychologically from the legacy of racism in all its variations.

Black females need a safe space to talk about and reflect on their families: the good and the bad, its African roots, and its contemporary troubles. Most are well aware of the proportionally high number of single-parent homes, mostly headed by women. Indeed, Black women are often left alone with the responsibilities of providing for children, emotionally, economically, and spiritually. The ability to find ways to adjust in the midst of difficult situations has been a strength of the Black community—of its women, in particular. Helping young women prepare for issues before they arise means taking a proactive stance against the forces that threaten to break down and destroy families and individuals. By bonding together, Black women will find more strength to not only endure but to thrive. The lessons in this unit will provide structured activities and opportunities for fellowship that will help to fortify physical, psychological, and spiritual endurance and bonding.

UNIT LEARNING GOALS
- Examine personal family structure and lifestyle.
- Develop an appreciation for their families and relationships.
- Practice spiritual ways of communicating in relationship.
- Gain a closer identity with African roots.
- Complete the That's My Sister heritage project (page 89).

Bible study for this unit can be Numbers 27 (the daughters of Zelophehad) and/or Ruth the (story of Naomi and Ruth).

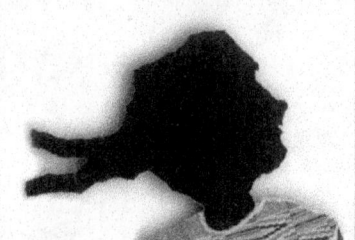

Opening Ritual With Prayer and Praise (page 46)

Celebration of Women (page 19)

1
My Family, Me, and You

Marian Wright Edelman has devoted her life to fighting for the rights and living conditions of children and families, especially the poor and people of color. She has advised legislatures and helped to develop public policy. She is often a singular voice advocating on behalf of children. Using the prayer on page 88 of Edelman's *Guide My Feet: Prayers and Meditations for Our Children*, begin the presentation by having a person read two phrases of the prayer. Read two more phrases between each paragraph and at the end of the biography.

LESSON FOCUS
The purpose of this session is to encourage young women to examine ways of being family—who belongs and how? Family origins will be investigated as well as ways of creating a sense of family connection that all human beings need in order to have abundant life. In addition to focusing on affirming the strengths of their families, young women need opportunities to make observations concerning its weaknesses and failures to provide appropriate nurture. By allowing the girls to openly address their situations, they can develop healthy and mature ways of looking at their lives. Writing in journals is a very important activity in thinking about family because many girls may have situations that they may want to confront but may not want to not openly discuss in front of a group. Mentors should be available for confidential sharing.

Introduce participants to the That's My Sister Heritage Project (pages 89–91). This is a research project that they will do away from sessions on their own time. It will be due the last session of this unit.

BIBLE STUDY

SISTER CIRCLES
Activity 1: Family Tree
For this activity, you will need the following:
Δ posterboard
Δ construction paper
Δ scissors, glue or glue sticks, markers

Divide the participants into small groups. Give each girl a sheet of posterboard and access to construction paper, scissors, glue, and markers. Ask her to design an attractive family tree. She may list all biological family members of whom she are aware. She may then include persons who may not be blood relatives but who are persons she considers family, such as play aunties, foster parents and siblings, guardians, and other extended family members. Older participants may have an advantage over younger ones in being able to map out their tree. (See A Traditional Family Tree Structure, in the margin.) Family trees should include as much of the following information as possible:

Father's Genealogy
- Father's full name, date of birth, place of birth
- Paternal grandfather's (father's father) full name
- Paternal grandmother's full name and her brothers' and sisters' names
- Paternal uncles', aunts', and their children's (cousins') names
- Paternal great-grandfathers' names
- Paternal great-grandmothers' names

Mother's Genealogy
- Mother's full name, date of birth, place of birth
- Maternal grandfather's (mother's father) full name
- Maternal grandmother's full name and her brothers' and sisters' names
- Maternal uncles', aunts', and their children's (cousins') names
- Maternal great-grandfathers' names
- Maternal great-grandmothers' names

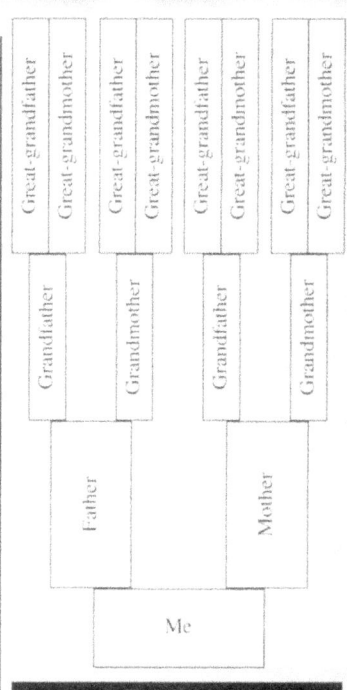

A Traditional Family Tree Structure

Activity 2: Stories About My Family
Each family has stories that have not been written down. Participants may write down some family oral history in their journals.

Then have the girls gather into small groups. Ask each girl to describe her family tree and her relationship to each of the people on her family tree.

Activity 3: You and Me
For this activity, you will need the following:
Δ photocopies of You and Me activity (page 80) for all participants.
Δ pens and/or pencils

Have the girls pair up. Each girl will use the questions on the activity page to informally interview her partner. This is an opportunity for each girl to discuss her likes and dislikes with her partner as well as to gather personal information about her friend.

GRIOT TIME
One Elder or Mentor should take no more than 10 minutes to talk about a time when family survival depended on unity.

CLOSING
After allowing time for participants to write in their journals, do the Closing Ritual.

Closing Ritual (page 47)

You and Me

1. I feel loved in my family when _____.
   When do you feel loved? _____
2. My position in my family is (youngest, middle, eldest) _____.
   What is yours? _____
3. One thing my family likes to do together is _____.
   What does your family do together? _____
4. One word I would use to describe my family is _____.
   How would you describe your family? _____
5. One thing to pray for my family right now is _____.
   How should I pray for your family? _____
6. What I like best about my family is _____.
   What do you like best about your family? _____
7. One thing I would like to change about my family is _____.
   What would you change about your family? _____
8. My favorite place in my house is _____.
   What's yours? _____
9. When I grow up I want or do not want to have a family because _____
   _____
   What about you? _____

What I Learned About Other Daughters of Imani

Name _____ Age _____
Address _____
Phone Number _____ Birthday _____
About Her: _____

Name _____ Age _____
Address _____
Phone Number _____ Birthday _____
About Her: _____

Name _____ Age _____
Address _____
Phone Number _____ Birthday _____
About Her: _____

Permission is granted to the purchaser to photocopy this page for use with DAUGHTERS OF IMANI: A CHRISTIAN RITES OF PASSAGE FOR AFRICAN-AMERICAN YOUNG WOMEN. © 2005 by Abingdon Press. All rights reserved.

2
Understanding My Family

The story of **Mother Clara Hale** is an inspiring triumph of mother love and care. As the girls listen to her biography, encourage them to think about the wonderful qualities that Mother Hale exhibited and how those qualities include love and nurture of family. Display artwork (preferably by Black artists) of babies and families in the presentation area.

Opening Ritual With Prayer and Praise (page 46)

Celebration of Women (page 23)

LESSON FOCUS
This session enables girls to go deeper into the meaning of family by thinking specifically about family needs and issues. What makes their family the way that it is? What is it that their families do very well? What is it that their families don't do as well? What strategies might help their families do things better? What are some of the things that all healthy families must do? How can families encourage and strengthen the girls in their process of development as young women? How can they give back to their families, and help their families to be better?

BIBLE STUDY

SISTER CIRCLES
Activity 1: Who Is Family? Mixed Media Collage
For this activity, you will need the following:
Δ posterboard
Δ magazines to cut up
Δ art supplies: construction paper, scissors, glue, markers, other items
Δ *Guide My Feet: Prayers and Meditations for Our Children*, by Marian Wright Edelman (pages 157–161)

Write out the response in the prayer in large letters, "Help us to welcome them in our hearts and communities." Before reading this prayer aloud, tell the participants to imagine the scenes described in the prayer as they listen. Prompt the participants to read the response at the appropriate places.

Give each participant a sheet of posterboard and access to the magazines and art supplies. The participants will create artwork based on the scenes they imagined. Read the prayer aloud several times as the participants work.

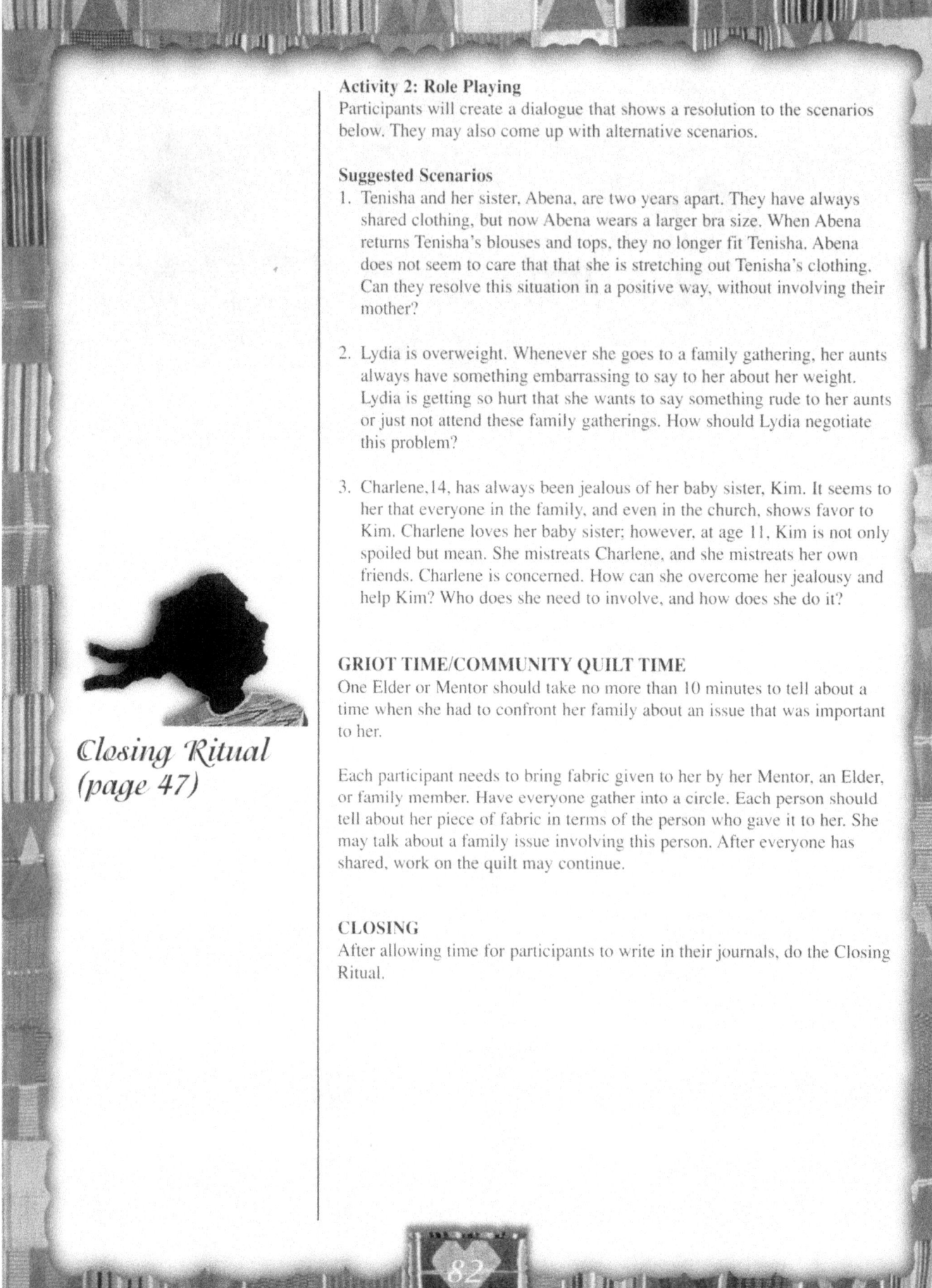

Closing Ritual (page 47)

Activity 2: Role Playing
Participants will create a dialogue that shows a resolution to the scenarios below. They may also come up with alternative scenarios.

Suggested Scenarios
1. Tenisha and her sister, Abena, are two years apart. They have always shared clothing, but now Abena wears a larger bra size. When Abena returns Tenisha's blouses and tops, they no longer fit Tenisha. Abena does not seem to care that that she is stretching out Tenisha's clothing. Can they resolve this situation in a positive way, without involving their mother?

2. Lydia is overweight. Whenever she goes to a family gathering, her aunts always have something embarrassing to say to her about her weight. Lydia is getting so hurt that she wants to say something rude to her aunts or just not attend these family gatherings. How should Lydia negotiate this problem?

3. Charlene, 14, has always been jealous of her baby sister, Kim. It seems to her that everyone in the family, and even in the church, shows favor to Kim. Charlene loves her baby sister; however, at age 11, Kim is not only spoiled but mean. She mistreats Charlene, and she mistreats her own friends. Charlene is concerned. How can she overcome her jealousy and help Kim? Who does she need to involve, and how does she do it?

GRIOT TIME/COMMUNITY QUILT TIME
One Elder or Mentor should take no more than 10 minutes to tell about a time when she had to confront her family about an issue that was important to her.

Each participant needs to bring fabric given to her by her Mentor, an Elder, or family member. Have everyone gather into a circle. Each person should tell about her piece of fabric in terms of the person who gave it to her. She may talk about a family issue involving this person. After everyone has shared, work on the quilt may continue.

CLOSING
After allowing time for participants to write in their journals, do the Closing Ritual.

3
Praying for One Another

Opening Ritual With Prayer and Praise (page 46)

Celebration of Women (page 27)

In her "Last Will and Testament," **Mary McLeod Bethune** prayed that African Americans would develop certain characteristics, including love, hope, confidence in one another, thirst for education, respect for the uses of power, faith, racial dignity, peace, and responsibility for young people. Present portions of Bethune's "Last Will and Testament" while a dancer dances. Someone skilled in movement should create steps that can be easily imitated by the participants.

Distribute a copy of Bethune's Last Will and Testament to each participant. Read it together. A Mentor will lead the exercise and ask the participants to create movements that visually portray Bethune's "Last Will and Testament." After giving the group an opportunity to listen and watch, repeat the presentation as the participants take part in the sections designated by the leader.

LESSON FOCUS

Participants will take part in interactive group activity that encourages bonding among the group. Participants will develop prayer partnerships within the group, and will make the commitment to pray for one another over an extended period of time.

BIBLE STUDY

SISTER CIRCLES
Activity 1: Let Us Pray
For this activity, you will need the following:
Δ index cards
Δ magic markers

Create a set of prayer cards to be distributed to the group. To create the cards, write on each card a prayer request, such as the following:

- Pray for the homeless.
- Pray for children in foster care.
- Pray for sick persons in hospitals and nursing homes.
- Pray for persons with AIDS.
- Pray for teachers.

- Pray for the President of the United States.
- Pray for the pastor of the church.
- Pray for the poor.
- Pray for persons in jail or prison.
- Pray for parents.

Other prayers may be used depending on the needs and interests of your group.

Have the students divide into pairs. Distribute at least one prayer card to each pair of participants. Depending on the size of your group, each pair may receive more than one prayer card. Ask the pairs to spend five minutes praying on their specific prayer concern(s). The pairs should pray orally, with each partner taking a turn to pray.

Activity 2: Prayer Bracelets
For this activity, you will need the following:
Δ elastic cord
Δ assorted beads: pony beads (assorted colors), heart-shaped or butterfly-shaped beads (assorted colors), and so forth
Δ prayer journal for each girl
Δ writing implements: pencils, pens, markers
Δ index cards
Δ chart paper
Δ markers

Participants will continue to spend some time talking to God, staying with their partners from Activity 1. Before the session, create a sample prayer bracelet. Be prepared to explain the colors. Each participant will make a prayer bracelet that includes a minimum of three prayers for her partner. She may include as many prayers as she desires. Play gospel or contemporary Christian music while the girls work. Allow time for participants to write in their prayer journal.

Ask the participants to share things that they might talk to God about. Record their responses on chart paper. Ask the participants the following questions:

- Do you ever pray for others?
- If someone asks you to pray specifically for something, how would you remember to pray for that?

Distribute prayer journals to each participant. (You may have included these in the Survival Kit you gave each girl at the beginning of the program.) Explain that a prayer journal is a place to keep a record of specific prayer requests as well as answered prayers.

Participants will develop prayer partnerships, making the commitment to pray for their prayer partner each day for one month. Ask each participant to write her name on a slip of paper and to fold it. Place the papers in a basket and mix them up. Hand the basket around again and have each girl take out one of the slips of paper. The name she has picked is her new prayer partner. (If a girl picks her own name, let her pick again.) The girls should not let anyone know the name they have picked yet.

To foster a sense of sisterly and spiritual bonding, each participant will make a prayer bracelet for her newly chosen prayer partner. There should be a minimum of seven different color beads. Write where all can see the information from the bead chart below. The girls should use heart and butterfly beads in the colors in the chart. Colors other than these may be used as the base color for the bracelet.

Have a prayer ceremony in which each participant will present her prayer bracelet to her prayer partner, sharing the prayers with the group. At the conclusion of the prayer ceremony, have the girls spend about 10–15 minutes with their prayer partner, sharing concerns and prayer requests. The girls should write their requests in their prayer journal.

GRIOT TIME
One Elder or Mentor should take no more than 10 minutes to tell about a time when someone prayed for her and how it affected her life.

CLOSING
Kentake Amanirenas of Meroe may be presented with an African dance of welcome. Then do the Closing Ritual.

Closing Ritual
(page 47)

Bead Color	Prayer
Red	To have the guidance and protection of the Holy Spirit
Blue	To live a life of peace and prosperity
Pink	To display a sisterly attitude to all females
White	To grow strong in Christ
Black	To grow strong in self-knowledge
Green	To always be willing to help those who are less fortunate

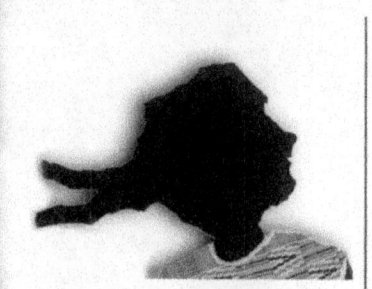

Opening Ritual With Prayer and Praise (page 46)

4
Heritage

LESSON FOCUS
This session acts as an introduction to African and African-American history.

Part 1 (*to be read aloud*)
Africa is the second largest continent in the world, after Asia. It is the most centrally located of all the world's continents. It covers one-fifth of the total land surface of the Earth and is almost completely surrounded by water. Its terrain includes vast deserts, tropical rain forests, huge mountains, and fertile grasslands. Africa has the longest river in the world, the Nile. Africa also has the largest desert in the world, the Sahara, which is larger than the size of the continental United States. Science holds that humankind, or homosapiens, first appeared in Africa more than 100,000 years ago. The oldest human remains continue to be found in eastern Africa. From that location, human beings spread throughout Africa and the rest of the world.

The ancient Nubian Empire is one of the world's earliest cultures. Its history goes as far back as 3100 B.C.E. The Nubian Empire was in existence for more than 3,000 years. The Nubian Empire (also called Kush, Cush, Punt, and Ethiopia) is mentioned several times in the Bible. The word *Nubia* comes from the word *nub*, which means "gold." *Cush* is the Hebrew word for Nubia.

Nubia, also known as Meroe, was located in East Africa, in today's southern Egypt and northern Sudan. It was rich in gold, ebony, ivory, and incense. Ancient Nubian civilization had a written language, Meriotic. Archaeology has revealed pyramids, temples, monuments, jewelry, and other artifacts. It had a powerful military and a sophisticated, diplomatic leadership role of Kentakes (Candaces), or queen mothers, who ruled the empire politically and militarily.

Between A.D. 700 and A.D. 1600, there were three main West African Empires: Ghana, Mali, and Songhai. While the slave trade and colonialism depleted and destroyed the political structures of much of Africa, the family systems of much of Africa, even today, resemble those of the Hebrew Bible (Old Testament) with clans, tribes, and patriarchs. Many African Americans are descended from the tribes that created the great civilizations of West Africa, countries now known as Ghana, Nigeria, Mali, Senegal, Angola, and so forth.

SISTER CIRCLES
Activity 1 for Middle and High Schoolers
For this activity, you will need the following:
Δ photocopies of the Tribal Characteristics handout (page 92)
Δ photocopies of the Map of Africa (page 34)

Δ list of the names of the countries of West Africa
Δ pencils

Have the girls study a list of the names of the countries of West Africa as well as the map with the countries labled. Distribute the Tribal Characteristics handout and pencils. Then give them the Africa map and have them fill in the names of the countries of West Africa on the blank map at the bottom.

Divide the girls into age-level groupings. Assign each group one or two area listings, and instruct them to prepare a presentation for the larger group. In their presentation, they will locate on the map their assigned area and use their creativity to describe to the other groups some of the characteristics of the tribes who live in their assigned area.

Activity 1 for Elementary Schoolers
Divide the girls into two teams. Taking turns, one member from each group is selected and blindfolded, given a pin, spun around, and pointed in the direction of the Africa map. The blindfolded person must then stick the pin to the map of Africa. The leader identifies the African country where the pin has landed and then the two groups race to find information about that country's characteristics in a dictionary or an encyclopedia. The first group to give correct information wins a point.

LESSON FOCUS
(*Play Negro Spirituals as this essay is read aloud.*)

Part 2 (*to be read aloud*)
(from *Young Lions: Christian Rites of Passage for African-American Young Men*)
In August 1619, a year before the Mayflower landed, an unnamed ship manned by pirates and thieves, sailed into the small Virginia settlement of Jamestown. The captain bartered his cargo for food and supplies. The deal was struck, and he sailed away, leaving behind twenty Africans, whom he had stolen earlier from a Spanish vessel bound for the sugar industry of the West Indies.

When Antoney, Isabella, Pedro, and the seventeen other unnamed Africans stepped ashore that day, it was as indentured servants. Indentured servants hired themselves out for a period of time in order to pay off a debt. Most Europeans who came to America were very poor (many were from debtors' prisons). This system of debt repayment was socially acceptable and widely used. After the agreed-upon period of time was over, the person went about the business of his or her life, with no shame for having been a servant.

The first generation of African Americans benefited from this system and was able to gain freedom. For the first forty years or so, the Black settlers could accumulate land, vote, testify in court, and mingle with Whites equally. Some held positions of leadership in the communities; some even acquired servants, both White and Black. Soon, however, because of greed, attitude shifted and opportunities closed. Slavery became the system of choice, because the growing cotton industry needed cheap labor in order to thrive. A whole economy based on the trade of human beings was established to supply the demand for workers.

Slavery was different from indentured servitude, because servants had rights—slaves did not. Servants could work their way out of their servitude, but slaves were slaves for life. Servants were given basic human respect; Black slaves were considered less than human. Africans were preferred to Whites and Native Americans because they were perceived to be stronger and had black skins, making them easy to identify as slaves. The culture and family systems of Blacks were ignored and destroyed in order to make cotton "King."

Activity 2: Heritage Discussion
Have the girls and women gather in small groups. Hand them questions based on the reading.
1. When did Black people first come to North America?
2. Why did they come?
3. Why do you think they were headed for the West Indies?
4. What is the difference between an indentured servant and a slave?
5. If you had to choose, which would you rather be?
6. How did Blacks end up being enslaved in America?
7. What makes one group of people try to enslave another?

GRIOT TIME
One Elder or Mentor should take no more than 10 minutes to tell about an experience of racism.

CLOSING
After allowing time for participants to write in their journals, do the Closing Ritual.

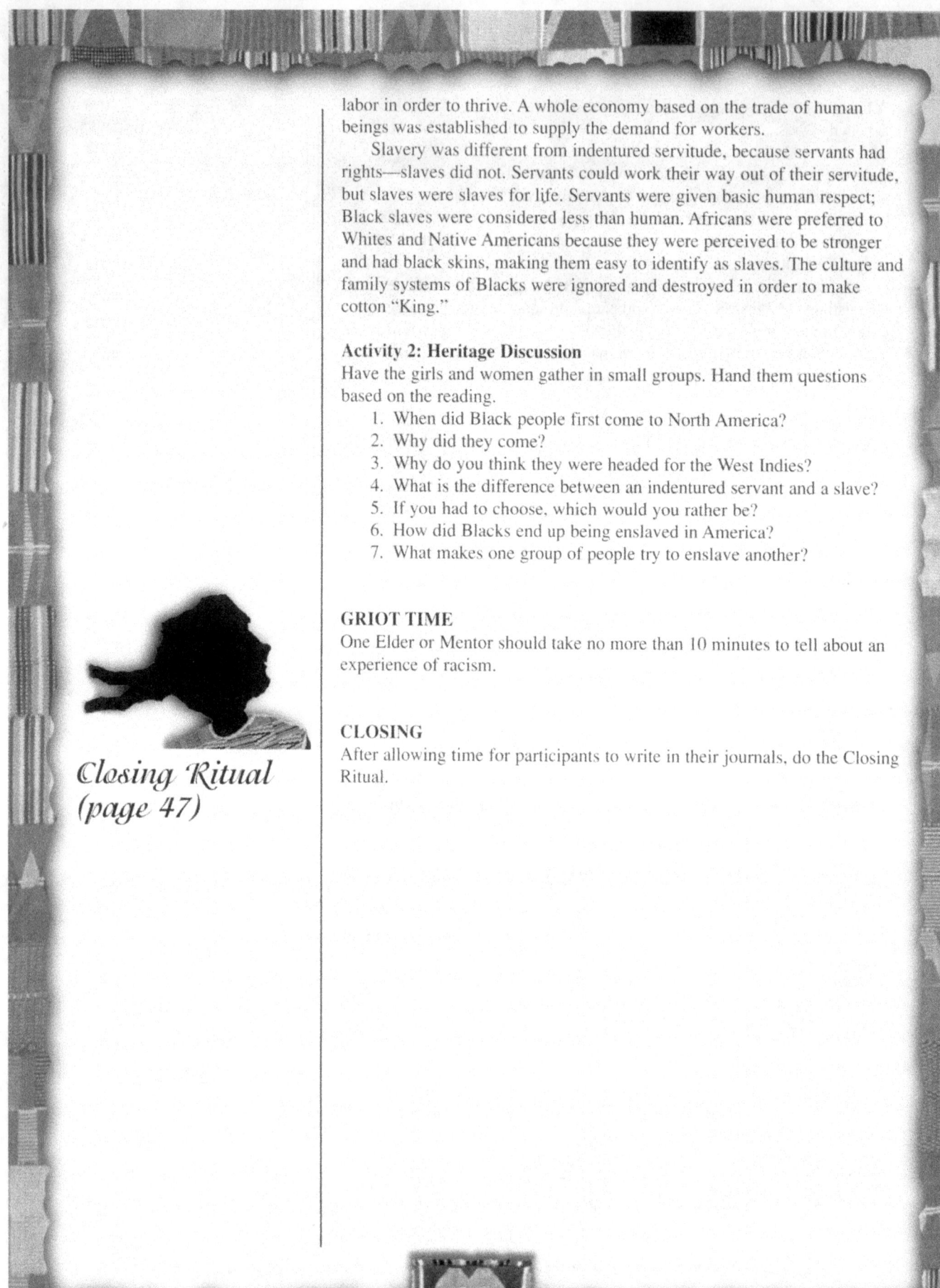

Closing Ritual (page 47)

That's My Sister Heritage Project

1. This project should be introduced during the first lesson of this unit and be completed by the last lesson. A point system can be used to identify those persons with excellent or satisfactory participation in the program.

Heritage Project	75 points
The Early Years	5
The Later Years	5
A Holiday Just for Her	5
She Deserves an Award	5
Cover Page	5
Creativity in Action	10
Sources of Information	10
Project Components	5
Birth Announcement	5
The Middle Years	5
Presentation	10
My Heroine's Lifeline	5
It's My Honor	5

2. Introduce the That's My Sister Heritage Project, by asking the participants to define the word *heroine*. Record their responses on the chart paper or chalkboard. After they share their definitions, explain that a *heroine* is "a female who is admired for the things she does to enhance the quality of life for others, or demonstrates excellence or greatness in a particular area." Ask the students to share names of African or African-American women they consider heroines and to say why the consider them thus.

3. Distribute the That's My Sister" Heritage Project (pages 90–91) to each participant. Read over the project, and answer any questions that may arise. Share and show some of the literary resources that are available, and encourage the girls to visit the library and to use the Internet and encyclopedias to find sources of information.

4. Tell the participants the date that the project must be completed and turned in. Before the end of the session, record the name of each participant and the name of the heroine they will research.

That's My Sister
HERITAGE PROJECT

SOURCES OF INFORMATION

To learn more about the heroine you have chosen, you will use many different sources of information. A good place to start is the library. There you will find biographies and autobiographies. A biography is a book written about a person's life. An autobiography is a life story written by that person herself. Other sources of information may include encyclopedias, videos, magazine and newspaper articles, interviews and the Internet.

Try to use at least three different sources of information. Write down each source and tell what the name of the source is, the date it was published; the publishers name and the date. If you do an interview, you will want to give the name of the person you interview and tell how that person is familiar with the famous person. If you watch a movie or video, write the name of the company that produced it. If you use the internet, please write the name of the website.

PROJECT COMPONENTS

Supply the following information about your heroine:
- —My heroine is . . .
- —She is my heroine because . . .
- —She is a heroine for her contribution in . . .

BIRTH ANNOUNCEMENT

Use your sources of information to find out the full name, birth date, birth place, and parents' names of your heroine. Create a birth certificate for your heroine.

THE EARLY YEARS

The early years cover birth through the high school years. Find information about her family, what influenced her growing up, and three additional facts about the early years of your heroine's life that you think are important.

THE MIDDLE YEARS

Find out at least five facts about the middle years of your heroine's life. The middle years are usually the years after a person finishes her education, begins her career, starts a family, and so forth.

THE LATER YEARS

The later part of life differs for many people. Write at least four facts about this time in her life. If this is not possible because your heroine is still relatively young, write about the accomplishments that made her famous.

Notes

Permission is granted to the purchaser to photocopy this page for use with DAUGHTERS OF IMANI: A CHRISTIAN RITES OF PASSAGE FOR AFRICAN-AMERICAN YOUNG WOMEN, © 2005 by Abingdon Press. All rights reserved.

PRESENTATION
After finding facts about your heroine's life, type the information. Remember to write in complete sentences.

MY HEROINE'S LIFELINE
Create a time line of important events in your heroine's life. Write the events in chronological order, with labeled marks on the line to indicate the years in which the event occurred.

IT'S MY HONOR
Heroines are often recognized for their achievements. Ways they are honored might include: monuments, holidays, awards, faces on stamps or money, books, songs. What special honors has your heroine received? You have the opportunity to create a special honor of your own. Write a letter to the President of the United States, telling how, why, and what reason your heroine should receive a special honor. In addition to writing a letter, draw a picture of how your heroine would be honored.

AN INTERVIEW WITH
If you could interview your heroine, what five questions would you ask?

A HOLIDAY JUST FOR HER
Imagine that a holiday has been declared to honor your heroine. Invent the name of the holiday and tell how people will celebrate it. Then be prepared to give a brief biographical sketch about your heroine at a national award ceremony. Your presentation should be no longer than two minutes. Write down the facts that you think the audience should know. Be prepared to speak in front of your group.

SHE DESERVES AN AWARD
Illustrate the special trophy or award created to honor your heroine. Inscribe it with words that tell something about your heroine.

SUMMING IT UP
Now that you've completed your research, answer the following questions: 1) What do you think was this person's greatest contribution or accomplishment? 2) When do you think this person made her greatest contribution? In what ways? 3) How do you think that this person has influenced the lives of others? 4) Do you think that you would have liked to meet this sister or to have her as a friend? Explain your answer.

COVER PAGE
Create an attractive cover for your project. Include her name and a picture if possible

CREATIVITY IN ACTION
Create an artistic presentation that gives us a visual portrait of your heroine. Use one or more of these ideas or come up with your own: Poster, sculpture, puzzle, mobile, diagram, word search, collage, model, brochure, game, puppet, diary entry, song, diorama, skit, video, commercial, poem, newspaper story, comic strip, mural, and so forth.

Notes

Tribal Characteristics

Many African Americans are descended from ethnic groups in West Africa. Regional areas include Senegambia, the Sierra Leone Coast, the Gold Coast, the Niger Delta, the Central African Coast.

Senegambia
SENEGAL, GAMBIA, GUINEA-BISSAU, MALI, GUINEA, BURKINO FASO AND MAURITANIA.

Wolof People reside mostly in Gambia.

Mandingo People's ancestors were associated with the great empire of Ancient Mali.

Dogon People are from Mali. Their ancestors had an excellent understanding of the solar system and the universe 700 years ago. The Dogon had detailed knowledge of a white dwarf companion star to Sirius, which was not visible to the naked eye, which means that they must have had some form of telescopes.

Sierra Leone Coast
SIERRA LEONE, LIBERIA, IVORY COAST, COTE D'IVOIRE.

Vai People are known as the only tribe in West Africa that has a written language.

Gola People are believed to be one of the groups from which the Gullah Sea Islands Peoples of Georgia and South Carolina are descended.

Grebo People are known for their world famous masks and for the men's and women's secret societies.

Gold Coast
GHANA, TOGO, BENIN

Ashanti People are the largest group in Ghana, and one of the few matrilineal societies in West Africa.

Ewe People, who occupy southeastern Ghana and the southern parts of neighboring Togo and Benin, where they speak European languages as fluently as their native languages.

Ga People are found in Southeast Ghana and Togo. Ga is the major language of Accra, the capital of Ghana.

Niger Delta
NIGERIA, CAMEROON, AND EQUATORIAL GUINEA

Igbo (Ibo) People are a large but widely spread population that inhabit both sides of the Niger River in Nigeria.

Yoruba People are located in southwestern Nigeria. The Yoruba developed a complex number system based on twenty. The Yoruba are also in Benin.

Hausa People are located in Northern Nigeria. The rise of the Hausa states occurred between A.D. 500 and 700.

Central African Coast
DEMOCRATIC REPUBLIC OF CONGO, CENTRAL AFRICAN REPUBLIC, CHAD, CAMEROON, EQUATORIAL GUINEA, SAO TOME AND PRINCIPE, GABON, ANGOLA

Bakongo People (a.k.a. The Kongo) dwell along the Atlantic coast of Africa from Congo to Angola.

Tikar People created a huge kingdom in Central and West Africa (what is now Cameroon) that lasted for three centuries.

Fang People are spread over a vast area along the Atlantic coast line of equatorial Africa and can be found in Cameroon, Equatorial Guinea, and Gabon, along the bank of the Ogowe river.

Permission is granted to the purchaser to photocopy this page for use with DAUGHTERS OF IMANI: A CHRISTIAN RITES OF PASSAGE FOR AFRICAN-AMERICAN YOUNG WOMEN, © 2005 by Abingdon Press. All rights reserved.

Unit 3
Health and Sexuality

This unit is designed to enable participants, at their respective age levels, to learn and to reflect on the physiological aspects of being a woman. Positive habits in the areas of healthy living, relationships, and sexuality will affect the level of success and happiness that these young girls will experience. Open discussions, pertinent information, and a loving atmosphere surrounded by affirming witnesses under the guidance of the Holy Spirit is the setting that mentors and elders are urged to create for the Daughters of Imani.

The issue of sexuality has historical, cultural, and mythological importance for all women. African Americans, however, in understanding the historical background in which the sexuality of Black women has been exploited, devalued, and abused, can move to a holistic strategy for confronting modern images of and behavior toward African-American women today. This holistic strategy is complemented by a spiritual recognition of the sacredness of the body, the temple of the Holy Spirit (1 Corinthians 6:19). Women are created in the image of God (Genesis 1:27). Therefore, by openly recognizing the historical and modern-day social, cultural, and political attempts to stigmatize Black women and their bodies, Mentors and Elders can enable young women to develop a Christian ethic of confrontation and refutation of negative forces. In being able to recognize and, in turn, confront distorting images of Black women through the power of the Holy Spirit, young African-American women can be empowered to overcome these negative images and thereby control their own destinies.

In this unit, participants will learn of healthful strategies in which to live, work, and take care of themselves. They will be encouraged to value their bodies as temples and to claim in themselves the image of the living God. Participants will practice recognizing and refuting negative images of African-American women in this society. The material will provide knowledge and insight on the status of the sexual health of young Black women today.

Mentors should consider acquiring *The Black Women's Health Book: Speaking for Ourselves* (see page 127). While some figures may be dated, Part II: "Tell the World About This" includes articles by Rev. Linda Hollies, Faye Wattleton, Marsha R. Leslie, and Marian Wright Edelman that are very relevant.

UNIT LEARNING GOALS
- Have the opportunity to confront personal views on sexuality and the body.
- Learn positive methods of caring for the body.
- Gain access to information concerning the health and sexuality of Black women.
- Understand that their bodies are temples of God.

Bible study for this unit can be Mark 5:25-34 (the woman with an issue of blood) and/or Judges 4:1-10 (the story of Deborah).

Opening Ritual With Prayer and Praise (page 46)

Celebration of Women (page 35)

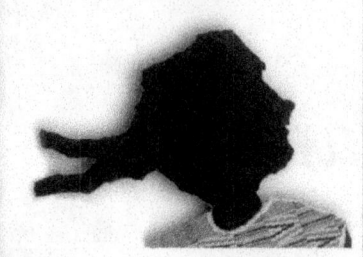

1
Self-Image and the Media

Mary Eliza Mahoney was a trailblazer for African-American women in the health profession. Her high standards and dedicated work ethic enabled her to become the first African-American registered nurse in the U.S. Accompany this presentation with a hospital scene skit. The team may also choose to use the "Mary Eliza Mahoney Monolgue," below.

Mary Eliza Mahoney Monologue
Until the late 1800s many American nurses were not formally trained. Doctors have not always been available to help the people, so nurses delivered babies and gave remedies for illnesses. In both the North and the South, many of these nurses were Black. African-American women have been nurses and midwives for most of their existence in the United States. Although nursing schools started opening after the United States Civil War, Black women were not allowed to attend.

However, I was an exception. I was the first African-American woman to graduate from a professional White nursing school. I first became interested in nursing when I acted as a midwife, a baby delivery person, at the birth of my younger sisters and brothers. I was the eldest in a family of 25 children.

When I was 33 years old, I was accepted at the New England Hospital for Women and Children in Boston, Massachusetts. This was the first American school to begin a nursing program. The head of the school, Dr. Marie Zakrzewska, was a firm believer in equal rights for women and for Blacks. My nursing course lasted 16 months.

Nursing school then, is not like nursing school now. I worked 16 hours a day, seven days a week. I washed, ironed, cleaned, scrubbed, and studied. This is what all nurses were expected to do. The classes and the physical work were so extremely difficult that only three women graduated out of a class of 40 students—two White women and I.

After my graduation in 1879, I worked as a nurse for 40 years. In my getting, I did not forget to give back. It was my mission to help people, while at the same time helping other women graduate from nursing programs. In 1936, the National Association of Colored Graduate Nurses established the Mary Mahoney Award. To honor my legacy and ceaseless efforts in the field of nursing and organization of nurses, an award is now given to those African-American nurses who contribute much to the nursing profession—as I did more than 100 years ago.

LESSON FOCUS
This session creates the opportunity for young women to learn more about healthful living and lifestyles. The Daughters will participate in activities that

will enable them to think about personal health and public health issues. They will learn how to glorify their bodies as gifts from the living God and as temples of the Holy Spirit. They will also learn about stress and emotional health issues, how to recognize and communicate those emotions to helpful adults.

BIBLE STUDY

SISTER CIRCLES
Activity 1: Statistics Worksheet
For this activity, you will need the following:
Δ photocopies of the Statistics Worksheet (page 96)

Hand out the Statistics Worksheet to the small groups. Ask the mentors and elders in each small group to have different girls read out each set of statistics and then to encourage the group to reflect on the discussion questions.

Activity 2: Gospel Hip-Hop Aerobics and Dance
Prepare girls and all participants ahead of time to bring comfortable workout clothing. Invite leaders who are familiar with dance and aerobic moves (do not have to be professional, just willing to dance and move!) Play upbeat music—hip-hop, r & b, even disco! The point is the move the body--get that cardiovascular motion going! Elders can take the opportunity to show dances they may have done in their day to the young girls, while girls can teach the elders new moves. Be sure to include upbeat heart rate activities, with the option of lower rate movement. Exercise for 20-30 minutes and have fun!!

GRIOT TIME
One Elder/Mentor should take no more than ten minutes to tell about an incident in which a medical situation was handled poorly.

CLOSING
After allowing time for participants to write in their journals, do the Closing Ritual.

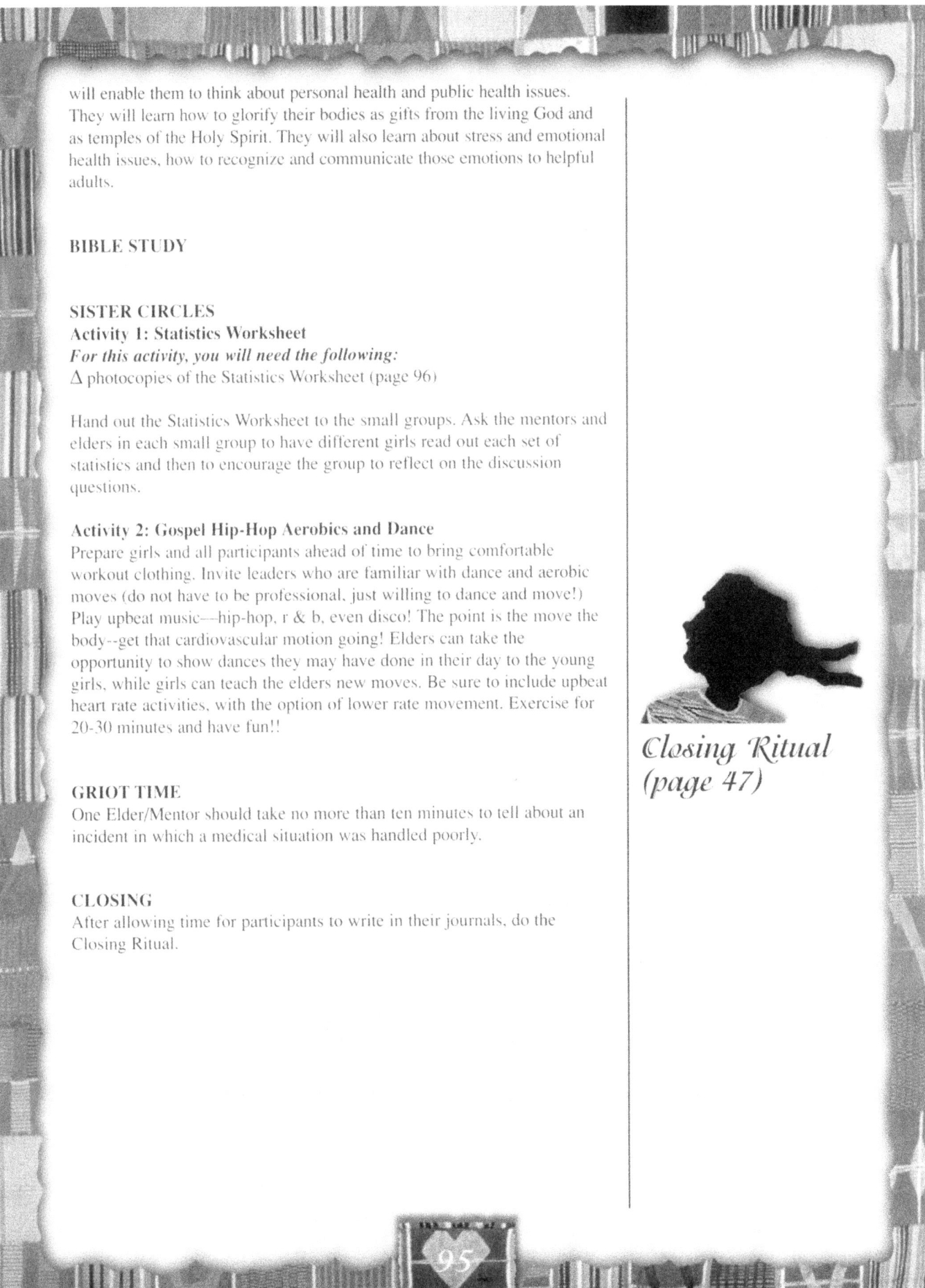

Closing Ritual (page 47)

Black Health Statistics

Importance of Exercise

A recent study from the National Heart, Lung, and Blood Institute (NHLBI) said that many teen girls aren't physically active, a warning sign that Americans' health is worsening. Nearly 60 percent of African-American girls and 30 percent of White girls studied do not exercise at all. And experts say that 60 percent of the American population is sedentary. The President's Council on Physical Fitness and Sports Report (1997) cites two research studies that suggest that higher female rates of athletic participation or exercise were significantly related to postponing first experiences with intercourse and lower rates of both sexual activity and pregnancy.

Sports Programs in Schools

Today, girls make up about 37 percent of all high school athletes; and one girl in three participates in sports. Despite these gains, girls' sports programs still receive a smaller share of resources than boys[*]; and girls have fewer opportunities to participate in school- and community-based organizations.

Signs of anxiety or depression in girls

Society's teenage girls seem to be facing a huge barrier to proper development and happiness. According to The American Association of University Women Educational Foundation (1998), adolescents' responses to questionnaires show that the adolescent years are a far more negative time for girls' mental and physical health than boys'. Parents and teachers may notice that young girls seem withdrawn, sad or apathetic, but attribute this behavior to female mood swings that are supposed to be normal during adolescence.

High Blood Pressure

Hypertension (high blood pressure) in African Americans is among the highest in the world. Compared with Whites, African Americans develop hypertension earlier in life and their average blood pressures are much higher. African Americans have higher rates of Stage 3 Hypertension than Whites, causing more complications. These factors are accompanied by an 80 percent higher stroke mortality rate, a 50 percent higher heart disease mortality rate, and a 320 percent greater rate of hypertension-related end-stage renal disease than seen in the general population (*blackhealthcare.com*).

[*]THE ATHLETIC EXPERIENCES OF ETHNICALLY DIVERSE GIRLS Jeanne Weiler Institute for Urban and Minority Education, Teachers College, Columbia University.
[*]ERIC Clearinghouse on Urban Education Institute for Urban and Minority Education.

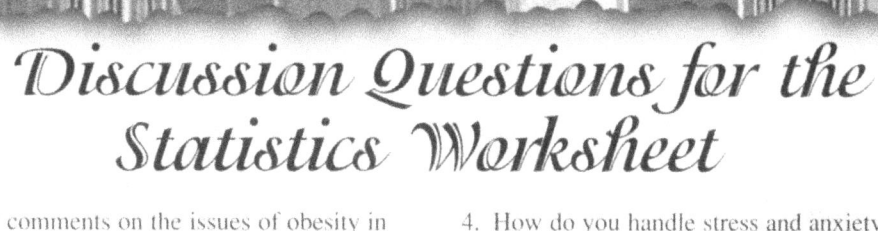

Discussion Questions for the Statistics Worksheet

1. Make any comments on the issues of obesity in African-American girls, sports programming for girls, depression and anxiety issues, common health concerns for African Americans (high blood pressure, diabetes), and the issue of insurance for women and children in the U.S.

2. Do you agree that African-American girls tend to be fatter or thicker than White girls? If so, why do you think this is the case?

3. What is sports programming for girls like in your school and community? Are you happy with available sports programming for girls where you are? If not, what can you, your friends, and parents do to change the situation?

4. How do you handle stress and anxiety? Do you feel you have people or resources to which you can turn when things seem a little too much to handle?

5. Why do you think African Americans suffer disproportionately from high blood pressure and diabetes?

6. What has been your experience with health care? Are you aware of the difficulties poorer people have in obtaining access to quality healthcare? Did you know that you and your friends can petition groups in your church and community to make concerns known to your local, state, and national legislatures?

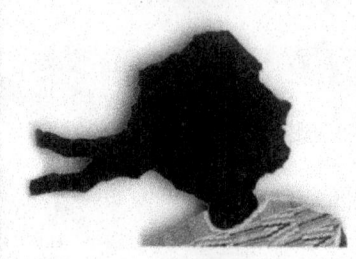

Opening Ritual
With Prayer and
Praise (page 46)

Celebration
of Women
(page 37)

2
Responsible Sexuality and Celibacy

In 1990, while she was still president of the Planned Parenthood Federation, **Faye Wattleton** wrote an article addressing the crisis in teen pregnancy that was facing America. Include a portion of her article, "Teenage Pregnancy: A Case for National Action" or "In a Family Way: Notes From a Black Teenage Mother," by Marsha R. Leslie, as part of this presentation. Both articles can be found in *The Black Women's Health Book: Speaking for Ourselves* (see page 127).

Leaders may choose to celebrate the Gbeto warriors who maintained perfect physical health as virgin wives who acted as bodyguards to the kings of Dahomey and Benin. Introduce them with a kick boxing or tae-bo demonstration. Use a video if no one with these skills is available.

LESSON FOCUS

Black girls are continually bombarded with American culture that is saturated with sexual images. Television programming, movie plots, billboard and print advertisements, music videos, popular styles are inundated with sex. Indeed, sexuality is offered as the lure in the marketing of everything from perfume to cars. The object of the sexual images is most often the female body. And, the message overtly and subtly proclaimed is that women, and certainly young women, are must be sexually alluring and desirable in order to have value in this society.

Christian women must learn to critically and consciously analyze a culture of promiscuous sex. They need to develop skills in order to process cultural images, make sense of them, and reject those that are potentially harmful. Creating an environment in which young women can openly discuss sexuality, life, and culture with responsible, nurturing and older Christian women provides a valuable opportunity for fostering positive values.

BIBLE STUDY

SISTER CIRCLES
Activity 1: Human Sexuality Quiz
For this activity, you will need the following:
Δ photocopies of the Human Sexuality Quiz (page 100)
Δ photocopies of the Suggested Answers to Human Sexuality Quiz (page 101)

Have the girls gather into small groups. Instruct the groups to respond to the Human Sexuality Quiz statements individually, then to discuss them as a group under the leadership of Elders and Mentors. The Elders and Mentors will use the Suggested Answers to Human Sexuality Quiz to help guide the discussion. Give them twenty minutes to do this in small groups. After the groups finish their discussion, hand out to each girl a copy of the Suggested Answers.

Activity 2: "Confronting the Big Question" Debating Skit
For this skit, you will need the following:
Δ photocopies of the Suggested Answers to Human Sexuality Quiz (page 101)
Δ other sources of information about human sexuality, including those from both secular and spiritual points of view
Δ paper
Δ pencils or pens

Divide participants into groups of three or more and dramatize this skit scenario: Renee is a virgin, but she is considering having sex with her boyfriend. Her friend Janet is sexually active and encourages her to get on the pill, use condoms, and just do it because it is the thing to do—especially if she wants to keep her boyfriend. Another friend, Prestine, tries to convince her to remain celibate for spiritual and physical health reasons. Janet and Prestine argue their points to Renee, striving to be the more convincing. (If there are more than three girls in a group, the group can divide in half, with one side arguing Janet's point of view and the other arguing Prestine's.)

Give the girls 20 minutes to prepare for the skit, formulating their arguments with the use of the Suggested Answers to Human Sexuality Quiz, any other sources you have provided for them, and their own experiences or knowledge of other's experiences. The groups may be as elaborate and imaginative as they wish as they compose a skit of about 5–7 minutes in length.

Allow the groups to practice their skits, then have them perform before the whole group. Then have the whole group analyze the different viewpoints and tactics used to convince the Renee of either side in each skit.

GRIOT TIME
One Elder or Mentor should take no more than ten minutes to tell about the onset of menopause.

CLOSING
After allowing time for participants to write in their journals, do the Closing Ritual.

Closing Ritual (page 47)

Human Sexuality Quiz

Read each statement. Write "A" if you agree, "D" if you disagree, and "W" is you want to discuss it further. Ask about words you do not understand.

1. _____ It is wrong for girls and boys to discuss sex with each other.
2. _____ It is OK for boys to tell dirty jokes but not for girls to do so.
3. _____ Girls reach puberty at a younger age than boys do.
4. _____ Single girls should not have sex until they are married.
5. _____ If you have ever had sex, you are ruined or spoiled.
6. _____ Oral or anal sex is not considered to be "real sex."
7. _____ After a few dates, a boy has a right to expect sexual favors from a girl.
8. _____ A girl does not have to tell a boy that he got her pregnant.
9. _____ A girl should have sex with a boy so that he will keep liking her.
10. _____ When a person feels excited around someone of the opposite sex, it is a good sign that she or he is in love.
11. _____ All sexual activity should be avoided until after marriage.
12. _____ Modern contraceptive measures guarantee that a woman can't get pregnant.
13. _____ Menstruation for girls is a curse.
14. _____ Most girls and boys practice masturbation at some time.
15. _____ Girls who refuse to have sex are not cool or hip.
16. _____ Sex between a man and a woman is essentially no different from two animals mating.
17. _____ God gave humans the gift of sex for the purpose of enjoying it.
18. _____ God ordained sex for the marriage relationship.
19. _____ Sexual intercourse involves not just two bodies but also the persons' thoughts and emotions.
20. _____ Menopause marks the end of a woman's sexual life.

Permission is granted to the purchaser to photocopy this page for use with **Daughters of Imani: A Christian Rites of Passage for African-American Young Women,** *© 2005 by Abingdon Press. All rights reserved.*

Suggested Answers to the Human Sexuality Quiz

These answers are to be used only as a guide in the discussion of the Human Sexuality Quiz.

1. It is always healthful for people to be open and frank about sexual matters in the right context and in a respectful manner.
2. It is inappropriate for anyone to tell dirty jokes.
3. Typically, girls do reach puberty at a younger age than boys do.
4. According to the Bible, single men and women should wait to have sex until they are married to each other.
5. A person who has had sex is not ruined or spoiled. Sex is not just about a physical encounter; there is a spiritual and emotional aspect as well. Even though one has had sexual activity in the past, if she or he genuinely repents to God and willfully changes her or his behavior, she or he is forgiven and becomes a "virgin" again by the grace of God.
6. Any activity that is physically intimate is considered to be sexual, or "real sex."
7. Regardless of the closeness of a relationship, no male or female ever as the right to expect sexual favors from the other.
8. Every situation is different in the case of unplanned teenage pregnancy; therefore, it is important to use Christian wisdom; discretion; and the guidance of responsible parents, guardians, and others.
9. Having sex in order to maintain a relationship is wrong. If sex is presented as the only option to maintaining a relationship, that relationship should be abandoned, because it will be damaging to the development of positive self-esteem.
10. Physical excitement for the opposite sex does not necessarily mean that the person is genuinely in love. There is a difference between purely physical feelings and feelings that involve the mind, spirit, and body.
11. It is biblical that Christians refrain from all sexual activity until marriage.
12. No modern contraceptive measure is 100 percent guaranteed to prevent pregnancy. Abstinence is the only sure prevention.
13. The notion that menstruation is a curse is an ancient prejudice that has been passed on to some people. Unfortunately, this prejudice starts with the Bible (Leviticus 15:19-24). Menstruation was created by God, and nothing God creates is cursed. The fact is that since menstruation is divinely created, it is a beautiful and sacred monthly event that signifies the female body's design as the instrument in which human life is conceived, nurtured, and supported.
14. Some people do practice masturbation individually.
15. Girls and boys who refuse to have sex are not "un-cool" or "un-hip" but are actually individuals who foster their own sense of self-worth and refuse to be pressured into doing something they do not feel ready to do. They are, in fact, the ultimate "cool" or the ultimate "hip."
16. Sexual intercourse between a man and a woman is a specially ordained activity designed by God and is meant for individuals brought together under the anointing of holy matrimony. Therefore, it is more sacred and significant than two animals mating together.
17. God created sex to be enjoyable and meaningful between two persons who are brought together in love and marriage by God's grace.
18. The covenant of marriage is exclusively the domain for which God ordained sex.
19. Because sexual activity is such a powerful act created by a divine and loving God, when two persons come together physically, the connection is not just physical but spiritual and emotional.
20. Menopause does not mark the end of a woman's sexual life, because God created intimacy to last between two covenanted partners throughout the lifetime of a relationship.

Permission is granted to the purchaser to photocopy this page for use with DAUGHTERS OF IMANI: A CHRISTIAN RITES OF PASSAGE FOR AFRICAN-AMERICAN YOUNG WOMEN, © 2005 by Abingdon Press. All rights reserved.

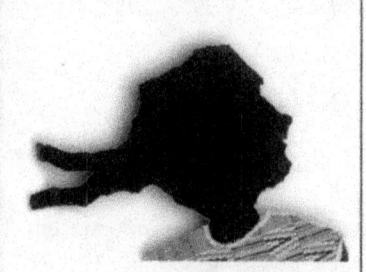

Opening Ritual With Prayer and Praise (page 46)

Celebration of Women (page 43)

3
Sexually Transmitted Diseases and HIV/AIDS

Dr. Hilda Hutcherson is a leading expert on female sexuality. Present her information with a backdrop of items for women's bodies. Cover a table with a pretty cloth and light a mild-smelling candle. Place tampons, sanitary napkins, lotions, bubble bath, skin creams, breast pads (for nursing mothers), fingernail polish, nail brushes, shampoos and conditioners, condoms, a diaphragm, feminine and underarm deodorants, make-up, facial cleaners, loofahs, (and whatever else you think of and feel is appropriate) on the table.

LESSON FOCUS
Most young people who enter into sexual relationships do so out of love, curiosity, or peer pressure. Two of the unintended results of sexual activity are pregnancy and sexually transmitted diseases. Information is presented in this session as a way to provide knowledge and insight as well as to create settings in which younger women speak with older women about these crucial issues. Gleaning wisdom and guidance from the Elders is just as important as getting the facts. It means a great deal to younger women striving to find their way for older women to share from the heart, with honesty, love, and concern.

The rates of HIV/AIDS and other STD infections in African-American women are quite alarming. African-American women are at the top of the list, proportionally, in the incidence of various infections, with HIV/AIDS a top killer of Black women ages 25–44. Additionally, women over 55 have one of the fastest growing rates of infection. In some African cultures, women are not allowed to say no to a man who demands sex, which leaves them vulnerable to sexually transmitted diseases. Violence towards Black women as exemplified by much in the hip-hop culture has its roots in a basic disrespect of Black women that permeates many social structures. Therefore, it is very important that these realities be addressed among Black women.

What Your Mother Never Told You About Sex* (see page 127), includes chapters that explicitly explore the sexual body, sex acts, sexual health and safety, lifelong sex, and sex problems. It answers questions that women have been afraid to ask about their bodies but need to know in order to become comfortable with their sexuality—and with sex. Elders and Mentors should review this material thoroughly before using it with participants.

Another resource, "Be a Force for Change: Talk With Young People About HIV/AIDS (Information Guidance to Get You Started)" (see page 127) is a 30-page pamphlet that contains chapters entitled "Parents' Primer," "Common Questions," "Starting the Conversation," "Deciding What to Say," and and "Information for Children/Teenagers."

The resource "Keeping It Real: A Faith-based Model for Teen Dialogue on Sex and Sexuality" (see page 127) is a course developed by the Black Church Initiative of the Religious Coalition for Reproductive Choice. The RCRC also sponsors an annual conference in July at the Howard University School of Divinity. The 2003 youth track of the conference included workshops entitled "Ready to Live: Legacy, How I'm Living," "Created in His Image: Who Am I?" and "Listen Up: Intergenerational Communication." (See page 127 for additional phone numbers and websites.)

BIBLE STUDY

SISTER CIRCLES
Activity 1: Sexual Activity Quiz
For this activity, you will need the following:
Δ photocopies of the Sexual Activity Quiz (page 104)
Δ photocopies of the Suggested Answers to the Sexual Activity Quiz (page 105)

Divide the participants into small groups. Hand out the Sexual Activity Quiz to all participants. Instruct the groups to respond individually to the statements on the quiz then to discuss them as a group under the leadership of Elders and Mentors. Elders and Mentors will use the Suggested Answers to help them guide the discussion. Allow 20 minutes for the small group discussion, then give the girls copies of the Suggested Answers.

Activity 2: Fact Sheet
For this activity, you will need the following:
Δ video of the movie *Brown Sugar*
Δ DVD player or VCR and TV
Δ photocopies of the STDs and HIV/AIDS Fact Sheet (page 106)

In 2002, the movie *Brown Sugar* was released. It is a romantic story that chronicles the beginnings and history of hip-hop music. Find the scene in which Sydney, a journalist, goes on a first date with Kelby, a basketball player. They end up having sex. Watch this scene with the participants. Hand out the STD and HIV/AIDS Fact Sheet. Read the facts aloud, then discuss with the girls the questions at the bottom of the page.

GRIOT TIME
One Elder or Mentor should take no more than 10 minutes to talk about an escape from a violent situation.

CLOSING
After allowing time for participants to write in their journals, do the Closing Ritual.

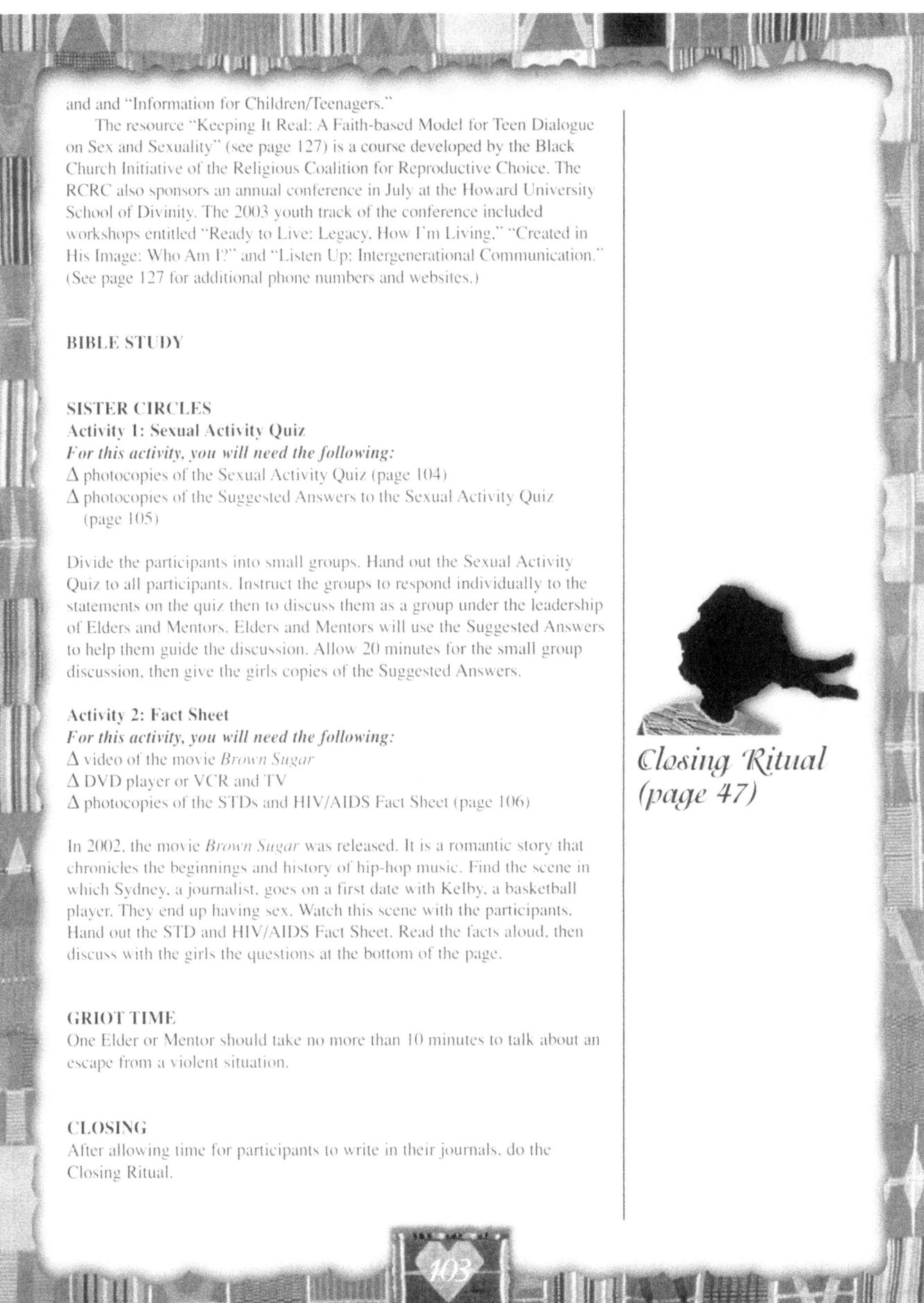

Closing Ritual (page 47)

Sexual Activity Quiz

Respond to the following statements by writing an A for Agree or a D for Disagree in the space provided. If you don't understand, write a W if you come across a word you don't know or need explained.

1. _____ A girl should not bring up the issue of having protected sex to a boy because he might become angry with her.

2. _____ A person should check out the sexual history of a potential sex partner in order to avoid getting a sexually transmitted disease.

3. _____ Sex is safest in a monogamous relationship.

4. _____ A person can get AIDS from physical contact from a person who is HIV positive.

5. _____ It is possible to get more than one sexually transmitted disease at one time.

6. _____ If a girl is on the pill, she cannot get sexually transmitted diseases.

7. _____ A girl should trust a boy to tell her whether he has sexually transmitted diseases.

8. _____ A girl should rely on the boy to have contraceptives and protection.

9. _____ Heterosexual transmission is the primary way African-American women contract HIV/AIDS.

10. _____ The only way a guy can get respect from a young woman is to physically and sexually dominate her.

Permission is granted to the purchaser to photocopy this page for use with DAUGHTERS OF IMANI: A CHRISTIAN RITES OF PASSAGE FOR AFRICAN-AMERICAN YOUNG WOMEN, © 2005 by Abingdon Press. All rights reserved.

Suggested Answers to the Sexual Activity Quiz

1. A girl should never feel so uncomfortable or afraid to bring up the issue of having protected or safe sex with a boy. If she does feel that uncomfortable or worries that the boy would get angry, irritated, or defensive, that is a good sign she should not be considering sexual activity at all.

2. When two people engage in sex, they are exposed to the other one's sexual past. Therefore, before any physical intimacy occurs, it is necessary to be thoroughly informed about that past. This happens best in the setting of marriage, when two individuals can come together, yoked as one, and know all about each other.

3. Sex is, indeed, safest and blessed in a monogamous relationship of commitment anointed by the sacred vows of holy matrimony and, as such, is ordained by God.

4. The only way to contract HIV/AIDS is through the transmission of bodily fluids, such as blood or semen, through physical sexual intimacy or the use of infected needles and other drug paraphernalia.

5. It is possible to be infected with more than one sexually transmitted disease at a time.

6. Oral contraceptives, or "the pill," is designed to hormonally affect the body to prevent pregnancy. However, the pill provides no protection whatsoever from the possibility of becoming infected with any sexually transmitted disease.

7. A girl should never assume that a boy will be honest or forthcoming about having a sexually transmitted disease. She must take it upon herself to become informed about his past. This means that she is concerned for her own health and her own destiny.

8. A girl should not rely upon the boy to obtain contraceptives, such as condoms or other forms of protection in the sexual act. She must take the active role in taking care of herself, primarily by seeking to refrain from all sexual activity until marriage and by avoiding situations that increase her vulnerability.

9. Today, heterosexual activity *is the primary way* that African-American women are contracting HIV/AIDS.

10. Respect is won by showing respect. Allowing a person to physically and sexually dominate another does not indicate respect, but fear and control. A woman does not respect a man who abuses her. Respect comes from fair treatment and affection. Therefore, no woman deserves to be mistreated or abused by anyone.

Resisting Pressure to Have Sex
Here are some things guys might say and ways you can answer:

GUY: If you love me, you'll have sex with me.
GIRL: If you love me, you won't pressure me.

GUY: Everyone is doing it.
GIRL: I'm someone and I'm not doing it."

GUY: If you won't have sex with me, I'll find someone who will.
GIRL: If you must, then do that.

GUY: What's wrong with you? Why don't you want to have sex?"
GIRL: Nothing is wrong with me. I want to wait.

Permission is granted to the purchaser to photocopy this page for use with DAUGHTERS OF IMANI: A CHRISTIAN RITES OF PASSAGE FOR AFRICAN-AMERICAN YOUNG WOMEN, © 2005 by Abingdon Press. All rights reserved.

STD and HIV/AIDS Fact Sheet

- In 2001, 75 percent of all reported cases of gonorrhea occurred among African Americans.
- The human papillomavirus (HPV type 16 herpes), which causes genital warts and accounts for about half of all cervical cancers worldwide, had the highest prevalence among African-American women.*
- Half of the 40,000 Americans infected with HIV each year are under age 25.
- African-American women account for 64 percent of those newly infected with HIV.
- As of Summer 2003, HIV was the third leading cause of death among all women and the leading cause of death among African-American women in ages 25–44.**
- In 2001, the chlamydia rate among African-American women ages 15–19 was nearly seven times higher than among White females (8,483 and 1,276 per 100,000 females, respectively).
- According to the study, girls who watched the most rap videos were more likely than the other girls to have hit a teacher, to have been arrested, and to have had sex with multiple partners. Sociologists have found plenty of evidence that the media, including music and television, affect the health, attitudes, and behaviors of teens.
- African-American women are more likely than any other group of women to be the victims of murder and other violent crimes.***

Discussion Questions

1. Why do African-American girls and women have such high rates of infection of sexually transmitted diseases and HIV/AIDS?
2. What are the dominant images of the Black woman in American society?
3. *Brown Sugar* is not a typical hip-hop movie. However, what images do you think hip-hop videos, along with the lyrics in the music that accompanies them, usually portray of Black women?
4. What do you think about Sydney's and Kelby's behavior? What could be some of the consequences? Do movies and television shows have an impact on the way that young girls see themselves and conduct themselves?
5. Think about the statistics that Black women have the highest proportional incidence of being the victim of violent crimes—homicide and domestic abuse. Is there a connection with the way Black women are perceived in the culture and the way they are treated in society? Explain.

* Advocates for Youth 1025 Vermont Avenue NW Suite 200 Washington, DC 20005 (*www.advocatesforyouth.org*)
** Healthcare Intelligence Network (*www.hin.com/edu.html*)
*** National Teen Pregnancy Prevention Research Center, Division of General Pediatrics and Adolescent Health, University of Minnesota, Minneapolis, Minnesota (*www.peds.umn.edu/peds*)
**** End Abuse Family Violence Prevention Fund (2003) (*endabuse.org*)

My Sistahs (www.mysistahs.org) helps young women of color address and learn more about sexual health.

Permission is granted to the purchaser to photocopy this page for use with **DAUGHTERS OF IMANI: A CHRISTIAN RITES OF PASSAGE FOR AFRICAN-AMERICAN YOUNG WOMEN.** © 2005 by Abingdon Press. All rights reserved.

4
HIV/AIDS 'The Truth Shall Set You Free'

Opening Ritual With Prayer and Praise (page 46)

Celebration of Women (page 47)

In addition to reading the biography of **Dr. Mae Jemison,** present a skit concerning the AIDS crisis in parts of Africa and the efforts being made to alleviate the situation. Note that before becoming an astronaut, Dr. Jemison was involved in world health projects.

LESSON FOCUS
This lesson will heighten the participants' knowledge and awareness of HIV/AIDS and other STDs and the effects of each upon the body and mind. It is designed to help participants distinguish between facts and misinformation about AIDS. It will also challenge them to share facts learned about HIV/AIDS with their peers.

SISTER CIRCLES
Activity 1: Discussion of HIV/AIDS
For this activity, you will need the following:
Δ photocopies of the HIV/AIDS Fact Sheet (page 109)
Δ index cards
Δ chart paper
Δ pens
Δ markers
Δ tape

Have the Daughters arrange their chairs into a circle. Give each girl three cards and a pen. Tell the Daughters to write on each card something they have heard about HIV or AIDS. Gather the cards, shuffle them, and give each Daughter three cards.

Then divide the participants into two groups. Give three sheets of chart paper, a marker, and tape to each group. One of the girls in each group should use the marker to divide the paper into three vertical columns and label them with the following headings: *true, false, don't know.*

Ask the group to sort their cards according to the truthfulness of the statement and then to tape each card under the appropriate heading.

Allow 20–30 minutes for this activity, depending on the size of the group. Be sure to allow time after the sorting to lead a discussion of the scientific, medical, and social issues raised by the statements on the cards and where they are placed. Use the AIDS Fact Sheet as resource material.

Explain that persons living with HIV/AIDS live every day with people spreading rumors and making judgments about their condition.

Ask: If Jesus met someone living with AIDS, how would he treat him or her? Allow participants the opportunity to share. Then hand out to the Daughters copies of the fact sheet.

Activity 2: HIV/AIDS Peer Education Tool
For this activity, you will need the following:
Δ photocopies of the HIV/AIDS Fact Sheet (page 109–110)
Δ photocopies of the Truth Shall Set You Free Creative Project (page 110)
Δ photocopies of the STD and HIV/AIDS Fact Sheet (page 106), which was given out during the previous session
Δ assorted arts and crafts materials: posterboard, drawing paper, construction paper, glue, magazines, crayons, colored pencils

Connect Activity 1 and Activity 2 by asking: Would Jesus have taught the truth about HIV/AIDS? Explain to the participants that Jesus expects us to do as he would do.

Distribute the HIV/AIDS Fact Sheet and the Truth Shall Set You Free Creative Project. Read over the work plan for the creative project with the students. Answer any questions that may arise. Have the students browse through the HIV/AIDS Fact Sheet, and answer any questions that may arise.

Participants will create a tool that declares the truth about HIV/AIDS to their generation. They may use these choices: poster, diagram, mobile, collage, word search, brochure, game, diary entry, mural, skit, newspaper story, video, comic strip, song or rap, commercial.

Be sure to allow time in upcoming sessions to for students to present their projects.

GRIOT TIME
One Elder or Mentor should take no more than 10 minutes to talk about how she cares for her health even as she lives with cancer or has a chronic disease such as hypertension, diabetes, severe asthma, lupus, arthritis.

Closing Ritual (page 47)

CLOSING
After allowing time for participants to write in their journals, do the Closing Ritual.

HIV/AIDS Fact Sheet

What is HIV?
- HIV is the virus that causes AIDS.
- People who have HIV in their bodies have HIV infection, or are HIV positive.
- *HIV* stands for Human Immunodeficiency Virus.

How do people get HIV?
- HIV lives in semen, vaginal fluids, blood, and breast milk of a person with HIV.
- HIV can be passed during vaginal, anal, or oral sex.
- HIV can be passed while sharing needles and equipment to inject drugs.
- HIV can be passed by needles used for tattoos and piercing or to inject vitamins and steroids.
- Health workers caring for people with HIV can get HIV from needle-stick injuries.
- HIV can be passed on from a mother to her baby during pregnancy, childbirth, or breastfeeding.

HIV is not passed by the following:
- Donating blood
- Having casual contact, hugging, kissing, sharing food with someone with HIV/AIDS
- Using telephones, toilet seats, towels, or eating utensils after someone with HIV/AIDS has used them
- Contact with tears, saliva, sweat, or urine
- Bites from mosquitoes or other insects

What should you do if you think that you are HIV positive?
- Get tested.
- Get treated.
- Get healthy.
- Get on with life.

Why should you say no to sex?
- You can avoid many sexually transmitted diseases.
- You will not have to worry about pregnancy.

How can HIV and AIDS be prevented?
- By not having vaginal, oral, or anal sex
- By not shooting drugs or sharing needles or syringes for any reason
- By avoiding direct contact with another person's blood

What steps can be taken to stop HIV?
- Get the facts:
  - Read about it.
  - Talk to someone.
  - Visit or call a local clinic.
  - Call the National HIV Hotline (800-342-2437).
- Decide to be safe:
  - Believe that anyone, including you, can get HIV.
  - Commit to being safe and healthy.
  - Tell someone about your decision and ask for his or her support.
  - Be consistent—act safely in every situation.
- Follow through:
  - Be abstinent.
  - Use condoms if having sex.
  - Be monogamous.
  - Don't share needles for any reason.
  - Get tested for HIV if you have engaged in any behavior that puts you at risk for the disease.

What is AIDS?
- *AIDS* stands for Acquired Immunodeficiency Syndrome.
- AIDS is caused by HIV.
- AIDS is not a single disease but a set of diseases that follows an infection that attacks the body's immune system.
- When a person has AIDS, his or her body becomes unable to fight off infection and diseases.
- AIDS will eventually end in death; there is no cure.

What are the symptoms of AIDS?
- Whitish coating or spotting on the tongue or throat
- Swollen lymph glands
- Unexplained fatigue, aches, and pains
- Heavy cough (often with shortness of breath)
- Persistent fever, "night sweats"
- Skin rashes or blotching of the skin
- Diarrhea
- Weight loss not due to diet or increased activity
- Decreased appetite
- Persistent yeast infection in women

How can one reduce the risk of AIDS?
- Be celibate or limit partners.
- Use condoms and practice "safer" sex.
- If you are an intravenous drug user, quit. If you can't quit, don't share needles with anyone.

Pregnancy and HIV
- Women who have HIV can give the virus to their babies through pregnancy, birth, and breast-feeding.
- If you have HIV, you can avoid pregnancy by using effective birth control methods, including a condom to protect your partner.
- If you want more information about HIV and pregnancy, contact your doctor or healthcare provider.

The Truth Shall Set You Free
Work Plan

You have the opportunity to create an education tool that declares the truth about HIV/AIDS to your generation. You may use these choices: poster, diagram, mobile, collage, word search, brochure, game, diary, mural, skit, newspaper, story, video, comic strip, song or rap, commercial. You may work with another person, depending on the project.

1. Study the HIV/AIDS fact sheets.
2. Think about the best way to communicate with your friends.
3. Use this page to
   a. Make a list of the materials you will need.
   b. Make a diagram of your project OR
   c. Outline the steps you need to take.
4. Gather your materials.
5. Be creative!

Unit 4

Social Grace

Social grace can be described as Christian charm. It is part of a person's way of being and personal style, be that person male or female. People develop, over the course of their lives, a way of expressing themselves through body movement, voice quality, facial expressions, and their sense of responsibility. Social grace includes doing and saying the right thing, at the right time and in the right way, the way that is most considerate of other people. Good manners and a graceful style affect one's ability to be more successful in the world as well as the quality of interaction with others. These tools are helpful in enabling a person to make a positive impression in various settings. They also help a person to give some idea as to her inner character. The ability to relate to others in a pleasant and warm fashion is an asset for all young people. In a world that glorifies in-your-face communication, underachievement, and lifestyles that emulate "The Simpsons," young women need to be reminded that graciousness is always appropriate. Graciousness includes being on time. Personal style includes thinking about future life choices and planning for those choices—just ask Oprah Winfrey or Star Jones. "Conduct yourselves wisely toward outsiders, making the most of the time. Let your speech always be gracious, seasoned with salt, so that you may know how you ought to answer everyone" (Colossians 4:5-6).

UNIT LEARNING GOALS
- Evaluate various styles of clothing and accessories, learning the appropriate contexts and settings for styles.
- Learn proper deportment for various settings, and practice these manners in various exercises.
- Think about career choices.
- Learn about time and money management.

Bible study for this unit can be Esther and/or Romans 16:1-2 (Phoebe).

Opening Ritual With Prayer and Praise (page 46)

Celebration of Women (page 51)

1
Character in Social Life and Relationships

Ida B. Wells-Barnett exemplified proper conduct and manners. As an African-American woman living in the late nineteenth and early twentieth centuries, she stood up and sat down for justice. She knew how to handle herself in a variety of settings. Pass around a picture of Ida B. Wells-Barnett (see the African-American Heritage Teaching Cards, referenced on page 127). Have a short discussion on her hairstyle, her posture, clothing. As her story is presented, encourage the girls to imagine how she was dressed, how she carried herself, how she spoke in the various settings in which she found herself. Give the girls an opportunity to imitate how she might have stood, walked, or her tone of voice.

LESSON FOCUS

Developing healthy and enjoyable friendships and associations are integral to the growth process. Navigating the various social settings in which people find themselves, conducting themselves appropriately, and making wise choices are life skills that must be learned. Older women interacting with younger women and dispensing wisdom happens through conversation, activities, and example. This session starts the ball rolling for thinking about social life, reputation, and relationships among women. Additionally, older women have the stories and the experiences of life to share with young girls as well as an understanding of what it is like to be young and testing the waters of life.

BIBLE STUDY

SISTER CIRCLES
Activity: Social Role Playing Activity
For this activity, you will need the following:
Δ chart paper
Δ marker

Divide participants into small groups and give each group one of the two situations on page 113. Ask them to role-play the scenario, finishing the story.

After each group has role played the scenario in front of the other group, engage the whole group in a discussion concerning the issues. Have the girls help you create a list of character traits on the chart paper. As participants discuss and resolve the situations that were presented, have them consult the list to see which of the traits are needed. Character traits include trustworthiness, responsibility, caring, respect, fairness, cooperation, generosity, kindness, courage, and honesty.

Situation 1
When you are with your girlfriends, one of them begins saying some very negative things about another girl. You don't know this girl very well and you

don't know whether what they're saying is true. Your friend tells you to support her in what she is saying about this girl to another group of girls who plan to go and confront this girl and lure her into a fight. You and your friend meet the group of girls who say that they are going to fight this other girl. As you are walking, you all meet this girl, who says that the things being said about her are not true. Your friend then begins to defend the negative things that were being said about the girl and contends that you know these things to be true as well. Your friend then asks you to collaborate the accusations against the girl, accusations again that you do not know to be true. What do you do?

Situation 2
There is a boy at school who is considered to be extremely cute. He is popular, and girls like him. For the past few weeks, he has been dating one of your friends on the cheerleading squad. You and this friend have known each other since third grade. One day, the boy approaches you and starts flirting. He says nice things to you, hinting around that he would like to take you out. You don't really respond because, on the one hand, you are flattered that he is flirting with you; but on the other hand, you feel guilty because you know that he is dating your girlfriend. You decide to ignore him.

The next day, you see him by the lockers; and he does the same thing. Again, you don't know how to respond. You see your friend at cheerleading practice, and she is talking about how much she loves her boyfriend and how sweet he is to her. The day after that, you see the boy coming toward you again. He is looking directly at you and has a flirty smile on his face. As the two of you approach each other, what do you do?

GRIOT TIME: THE IMPORTANCE OF CHARACTER
In the large group, 3–5 Elders or Mentors will tell personal stories of real-life incidents concerning issues of character. *Character* has been defined as "having qualities of trustworthiness, honesty, responsibility, cooperation, caring, generosity, kindness, respect, fairness, and courage." Mentors and Elders must prepare before the lesson, thinking of situations that have happened in their lives—going as far back as possible, involving social relationships. Their friendships and interactions with their peers is the social theme that is emphasized. They may want to tell about how they fought with a best friend and how they were reconciled, when a good friend stole a boyfriend, an experience of being rejected by the crowd, going to their first prom and trying to decide on a date, and so forth. This is so the young girls can bond with the older women through stories to which young women can relate.

After testimony and discussion, participants may then write in their journals any personal reflections or thoughts concerning character. They may use the list to help them think about areas in which they may need growth.

COMMUNITY QUILT
For this activity, you will need the following:
Δ fabric brought by each participant, given by her mentor, another elder, or a family member
Δ other quilting materials, such as needles and thread

While sitting in a circle, each person tells about her fabric, in terms of the person who gave it to her, lifting up some of the positive character traits of her mentor. After sharing, work on the quilt may continue.

CLOSING
Gather to do the Closing Ritual.

- Character Education Partnership
  1600 K Street, NW, #501,
  Washington, DC 20006
  800-988-8081
- Character Development Group
  P.O. Box 9211 Chapel Hill, NC
  27515-9211
  919-967-2110

Closing Ritual (page 47)

Opening Ritual With Prayer and Praise (page 46)

Celebration of Women (page 55)

2
Table Hospitality

To be National Security Advisor of the United States is to hold one of the most strategic and influential positions in the world. In this position, **Dr. Condoleezza Rice** had many opportunities to exhibit grace in difficult situations. In January 2005, Dr. Rice became Secretary of State in President George W. Bush's second cabinet. She is the first Black woman and second woman U.S. Secretary of State. Dr. Rice's mentor and career booster during her early college years was Josef Korbel, father of the first woman Secretary of State, Madeleine Albright, of the Clinton Administration. Dr. Rice's first task as Secretary of State will be to broker peace between Israelis and Palestinians and to facilitate a democratic process in the West Bank. No doubt her sense of decorum and grace will be an asset. Present her life as if facing the challenges of a press conference.

LESSON FOCUS

Life offers people many diverse settings in which to interact with others. While the rules of conduct may be different for a football game than for a church service or a museum visit, a person's sense of worth comes through by the way she handles herself no matter where she is. This session will help young women be graceful in a setting with which most people are confronted often—eating in community. Meals are shared frequently at church, in the business arena, and among friends.

There is an art to preparing, serving, and being served food. There is an art to communicating at the table. Jesus was concerned about table manners. Stories by and about Jesus deal with when to prepare food (Mark 14:12-16), who comes to the table (Matthew 9:9-13), and how (Luke 9:10-17). There are even stories about when not to eat (Matthew 12:1-8). Jesus commended Mary for her gracious and generous act of anointing his feet at the dinner table (John 12:1-8). More important than any tradition or rule of etiquette is the spirit with which hospitality is given and received.

BIBLE STUDY

SISTER CIRCLES
Activity/Griot Time: Graceful Dining
For this activity, you will need the following:
Δ food for a meal
Δ recipes
Δ kitchen utensils, pots, and pans
Δ table items, including table linens, dinnerware, silverware, centerpieces

Soul Food is a movie that shows how a family preserved its unity through a tradition of eating dinner together on Sundays. Elders or Mentors may want to review this movie and choose a portion (10 minutes) of it to use as an introduction to this activity.

Participants will prepare a simple meal, serve it, set the table, and eat together. They will practice cleanliness, cooperation, conversation, and civility. Elders and Mentors will need to choose the menu ahead of time. In preparation, participants may need to be taught how to hand off sharp knives (handle toward the recipient) and other kitchen safety issues. The meal may be based on a business lunch, a conference banquet, a church fellowship, or a meal between friends.

There are two basic rules that apply to all situations: 1) make others comfortable; 2) enjoy your food and eat it safely.

GRIOT TIME
For this activity, you will need the following:
Δ spirituals, jazz, and classical music on CD or audiocassette
Δ CD or audiocassette player

Elders or Mentors may share words of wisdom and life experiences as the meal is being prepared. At the table, the goal is for all to share equally and to enjoy one another's company. Play spirituals, jazz, and classical music during this entire activity. Table talk may include information about the music. Encourage the participants to follow good table manners. Participants may benefit from having guidelines that the Council of Women can create, based on the list provided.

CLOSING
After dinner, do the Closing Ritual.

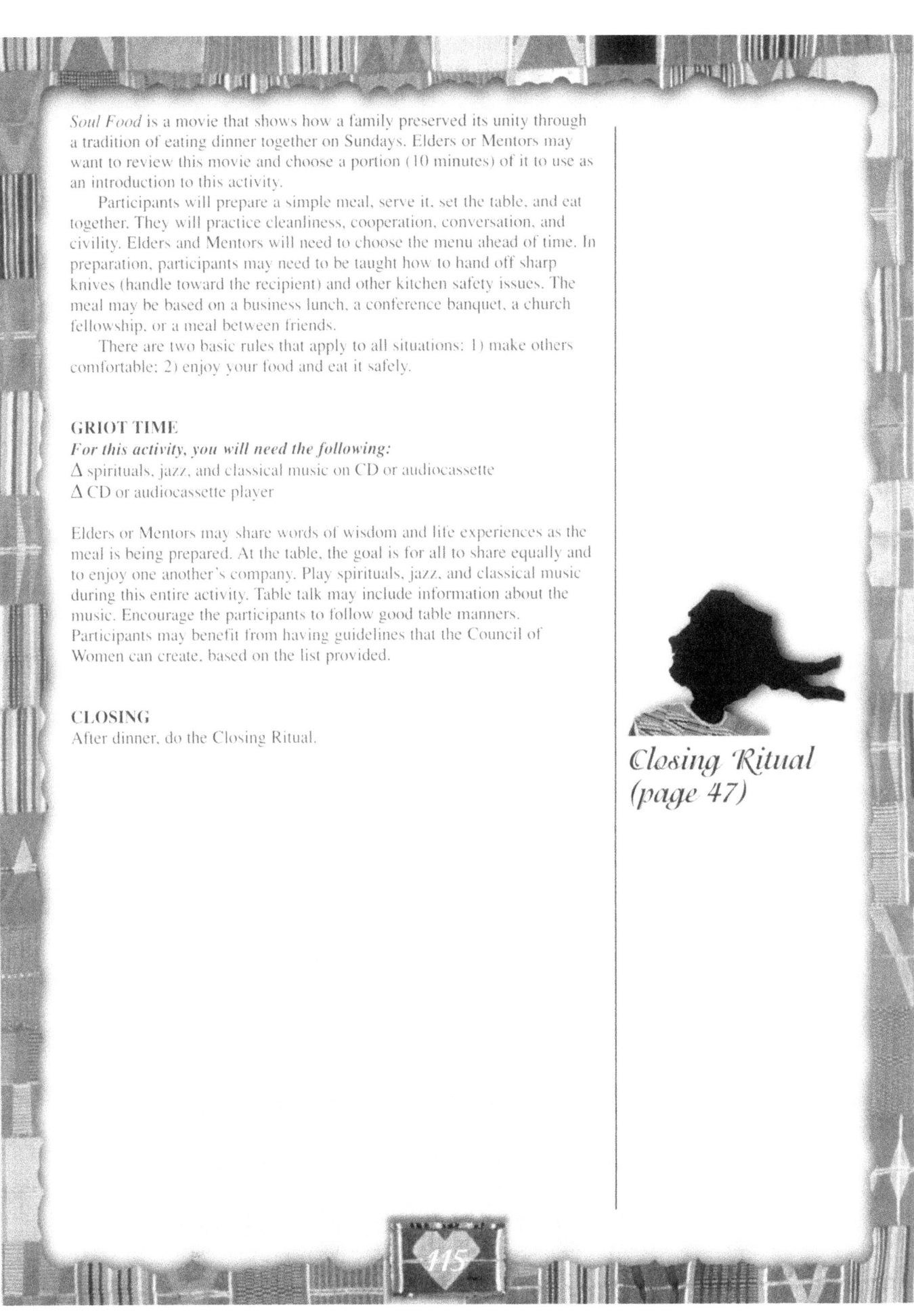

Closing Ritual (page 47)

Table Manner Guidelines

1. Eat slowly. Let your taste buds connect with what is in your mouth.

2. Put your utensil down between bites.

3. Finish chewing and swallowing before speaking.

4. Break your bread into small pieces. Sandwiches should be cut before being served.

5. Before you take each bite, cut meat and large pieces of vegetable into small enough pieces to chew easily.

6. Distract persons who are eating too fast by engaging them in topics that hold their interest.

7. Refrain from reaching across others to grab a dish or condiment. Ask for what is needed to be passed to you.

8. Avoid hunching over the table, and keep your elbows to your sides.

9. Put a napkin in your lap and use it when necessary.

10. Speak in conversational tones to persons close by.

11. Listen when someone is speaking to you.

12. Say please and thank you.

3
Beauty and Bounty

Madam C.J. Walker was an entrepreneur and beauty specialist. Put up a poster with Madame Walker's picture. Use this quotation to introduce Madame Walker: "I am a woman who came from the cotton fields of the South. From there, I was promoted to the washtub. From there, I was promoted to the cook kitchen. And from there, I promoted myself into the business of manufacturing hair goods and preparations.... I have built my own factory on my own ground."—Madam Walker, 1912, National Negro Business League Convention.

Display beauty products for Black women and the artwork (preferably by Black artists) that shows the diversity of beauty in African-American women.

LESSON FOCUS

African-American girls are bombarded with images telling them how they are supposed to look, what they are supposed to wear, and what style they are supposed to exude. It is important during the period of adolescence that a healthy self-regard develops with regard to physical appearance. However, many African-American girls develop negative perceptions of themselves. They may not like their size or body shape. They may not be happy with the texture of their hair or their skin tone or color. They may not like their facial features. Too often, African-American girls and women do not think that they are beautiful, an easy conclusion to reach due to society's European perceptions of beauty.

This session has a two-pronged focus. Like Madam Walker, women should not only be concerned with outward appearance but also about becoming women of substance. Having confidence in appearance is an important aspect of gaining the bounty of life. Personal style has an affect on job and career opportunities. Personal style should include making preparation to move forward in life. Like Madam Walker, participants must learn to promote themselves on their own terms.

BIBLE STUDY

SISTER CIRCLES
Activity 1: Images of Beauty (Part 1)
For this activity, you will need the following:
Δ fashion, hair, celebrity, and teen magazines
Δ clothing catalogs
Δ magazines and books that have images of women in them who are stereotypically unattractive

Opening Ritual With Prayer and Praise (page 46)

Celebration of Women (page 59)

Divide the participants into small groups. Give the groups the magazines and catalogs. Ask the groups to review the hairstyles and clothing styles and trends. Also have them analyze all of the images of women. Have them discuss why certain images are considered beautiful. Have them compare the "beautiful" images with other images, from magazines or books, that some consider stereotypically unattractive. Compare and contrast the images. Discuss which styles are appropriate for a job or school interview.

Activity 1: Images of Beauty (Part 2)
For this activity, you will need the following:
Δ pencils or pens

Participants will write in their journals, choosing to answer one of two questions:
　　A. I know that I am beautiful because_____.
　　B. Sometimes, I don't feel confident in my appearance because ____.

Give the girls a minute or two to answer the question, then have them come to together in age-level small groups led by Mentors and Elders to share their writings (optional). If girls don't feel comfortable sharing their writings, they may share experiences about issues regarding skin color, hair, body size, features, and so forth and tell how those situations affected their ideas about beauty.

Activity 2 (Part 1: Moving Toward Bounty)
For this activity, you will need the following:
Δ photocopies of the Career ABCs handout (page 119)
Δ chart paper
Δ markers

Have the group work together to list as many careers or occupations as they can for each letter of the alphabet. Write the list on chart paper. Take time to describe each vocation as it is mentioned to be sure that everyone understands what it is. Then distribute the handout, and have each participant choose two jobs from the list for which to "interview" for a job or college major.

Activity 2 (Part 2: Mock Interview)
Δ photocopies of the Interview Questions (page 120)

Pair up two young women to engage in a mock interview. One girl is the job applicant or college seeker, and the other is the employer or college administrator. Each "applicant" decides whether she wants her mock interview to be for a job or to get into college. After the first interview, the pair switches roles and interviews again.

GRIOT TIME
One Elder or Mentor should take no more than 10 minutes to tell about how she made a career decision.

CLOSING
After allowing time for participants to write in their journals, do the Closing Ritual.

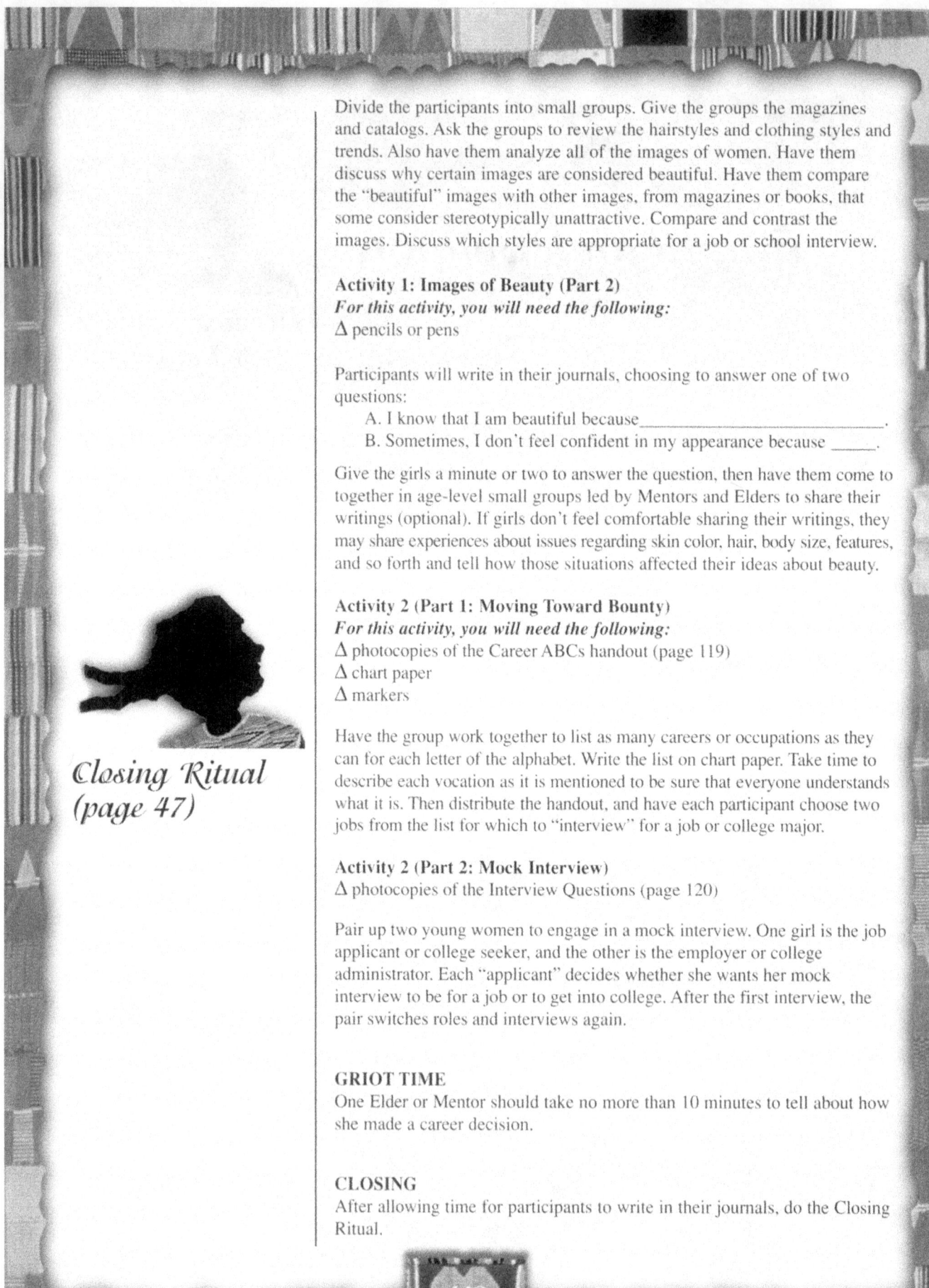

Closing Ritual (page 47)

Career ABCs Worksheet

A _____ _____

B _____ _____

C _____ _____

D _____ _____

E _____ _____

F _____ _____

G _____ _____

H _____ _____

I _____ _____

J _____ _____

K _____ _____

L _____ _____

M _____ _____

N _____ _____

O _____ _____

P _____ _____

Q _____ _____

R _____ _____

S _____ _____

T _____ _____

U _____ _____

V _____ _____

W _____ _____

X _____ _____

Y _____ _____

Z _____ _____

Permission is granted to the purchaser to photocopy this page for use with DAUGHTERS OF IMANI: A CHRISTIAN RITES OF PASSAGE FOR AFRICAN-AMERICAN YOUNG WOMEN. © 2005 by Abingdon Press. All rights reserved.

Interview Questions

Tell me about yourself.

Tell me about one of your major accomplishments.

Tell me about your strengths and weaknesses.

Are you able to take instructions from a supervisor?

Are you unemployed right now? If so, why?

How well did you do in school?

Why did you leave your last job?

What were your favorite subjects in school?

How do you respond to criticism?

Do you consider yourself successful or unsuccessful? Why?

What are your long-term goals?

What was the last book you read? movie you saw?

What do you like to do in your spare time?

What interests do you have?

Are you creative? Explain.

Are you a leader? Explain.

Do you have any questions?

Why do you want this job (or to come to this school)?

Why should we hire you (or accept you at our college)?

Permission is granted to the purchaser to photocopy this page for use with DAUGHTERS OF IMANI: A CHRISTIAN RITES OF PASSAGE FOR AFRICAN-AMERICAN YOUNG WOMEN, © 2005 by Abingdon Press. All rights reserved.

4
Time and Money Management

In making this presentation about **Maggie Lena Walker,** create a display of calendars, personal planners, banking materials, accounting books, investment items, and anything else having to do with money and time management.

LESSON FOCUS
Participants will discuss the importance of having a time management plan that promotes physical, mental-emotional, financial, social, and spiritual well-being. How we handle business and budgetary matters is indicative of the health of the whole self as well. Participants will be introduced to the topic of time management. They will be given the opportunity to examine how they spend their time and money. They will be encouraged to engage in activities that promote a balanced attitude toward the resources of time and money.

SISTER CIRCLES
Activity 1: Concentration/A Time for Everything
For this activity, you will need the following:
Δ index cards
Δ rubber bands
Δ prizes (optional)

Opening Ritual With Prayer and Praise (page 46)

Celebration of Women (page 63)

Create before the session, a set of "A Time for Everything Cards" for each pair of participants. (At right are a list of the various "times.") Write one time phrase on each card or use a computer to print out the phrases on labels. Paste the phrases onto the index cards. There will be 28 cards in a set. Shuffle each set of cards so that they will be in random order. Then put a rubber band on the sets too keep them together.

If at session time you have more pairs of participants than sets of cards, have the participants divide into groups of three or four, instead.

Divide the participants into groups of two, three, or four, depending on the number of girls and sets of cards you have made. Give each group a set of cards.

Before beginning this game of concentration, introduce the concept of time. Ask the participants

A time to be born	A time to die
A time to plant	A time to uproot
A time to kill	A time to heal
A time to tear down	A time to build
A time to weep	A time to laugh
A time to mourn	A time to dance
A time to scatter stones	A time to gather stones
A time to embrace	A time to refrain
A time to search	A time to give up
A time to keep	A time to throw away
A time to tear	A time to mend
A time to be silent	A time to speak
A time to love	A time to hate
A time for war	A time for peace

to give their definitions of time. Explain to them that time is a definite moment, hour, or period. Read aloud Ecclesiastes 3:1 (There is a time for everything, and a season for every activity under heaven.)

Have the pairs or small groups spread their cards face down (blank side up) on a table. Group members will take turns turning over two cards, in the hope of finding a matched pair. If a player does not find a match, she replaces the cards face down on the table; and the next girl takes her turn. If the player does find a match, she takes the two cards, reads them to the group, and keeps them. She also gets another turn.

The game continues until all of the cards have been matched. The player with the most cards is the winner. You may award her with a prize if you desire.

After all of the games have ended, reassemble the large group. Read aloud all of the time phrases. Encourage the participants to think of rhythms that will accompany a new reading of the time phrases. Allow time for the girls to create a step or clapping routine. Then let them perform the routine as they recite the time phrases themselves.

Activity 2: How to Plan, What to Plan, How to Do (Part 1)
For this activity, you will need the following:
Δ paper
Δ pens or pencils

Briefly discuss information concerning mental-emotional, physical, financial, family/social, and spiritual health. Use these definitions or recruit several persons who have an expertise in these matters to give a 5-minute exercise or presentation on these five categories. (The facilitator may choose to write the definitions on chart paper for the participants to see.)

Mental-emotional health is the condition of a person's mind and the way a person expresses feelings and thoughts. A well-conditioned mind helps promote a well-conditioned body. Reading, having challenging conversations, and learning new things help keep the mind in good condition. Taking the time to understand one's own feelings, expressing these feelings in appropriate ways, and developing positive self-esteem are ways to keep good emotional health.
Physical health is the condition of a person's body. Eating healthful meals, getting exercise, and proper sleep are examples of ways to keep the body in good condition.
Financial health is the condition of a person's understanding of economics and how to use money to maintain control of one's life or business.
Family/social health is the condition of a person's relationships with others. Good listening and communication skills are key in keeping family/social health.
Spiritual health is the way one's purpose and meaning in life contributes to a sense of well-being. A person promotes spiritual health through prayer, worship, Bible study, and showing concern for others.

Ask the participants to tell about one activity in which they participate that promotes each area of health. Distribute paper to the participants. Have them list on the paper the activities in which they participated yesterday.

Participants should try to remember everything, beginning with when they got out of bed in the morning until they went to bed at night.

Next to each activity, they should write at least one of the following:
- *ME* if the activity promoted mental or emotional health
- *P* for physical health
- *F* for financial
- *SF* for social/family health
- *SP* for spiritual health

Have the students identify how much time they spend in each area of health and rank each area from most time spent to least time spent, with 5 being most and *1* being least.

Then the participants share their results with the group. Have them identify what areas they need to spend more or less time. Participants may offer suggestions to their peers of ways to spend their time wisely in each area of health. Examples: to improve mental-emotional health—read a book, play a board game; to improve financial health—collect loose change in the house and save it in a jar; to improve social/family health—talk to your family about your day or visit an elderly neighbor; to improve physical health—eat raw fruit and vegetables or take a walk; to improve spiritual health—pray or listen to music with a positive message.

Activity 2: How to Plan, What to Plan, How to Do (Part 2)
For this activity, you will need the following:
Δ photocopies of the Time/Money Management Plan
Δ pens or pencils

Distribute the Time/Money Management Plan. Have the students create a plan for the next three days. Their plan should be based on their daily activities and plans as well as on how they use money (even if it is just buying a bag of potato chips).

Invited guests, Mentors, or Elders may teach the following:
- Discuss how to develop a budget, use coupons, get freebies, find the best buy for your money.
- Discuss how to establish a savings account and why it is important.
- Identify the purposes and uses of a checking account.
- Discuss the importance of building the economic power of our Black communities

GRIOT TIME
One Elder or Mentor (this can be the same person who teaches about organizing finances) should take no more than 10 minutes to tell about earning money for the first time, opening a bank account, missing an important appointment, or how she handled a budgetary concern.

CLOSING
After allowing time for participants to write in their journals, do the Closing Ritual.

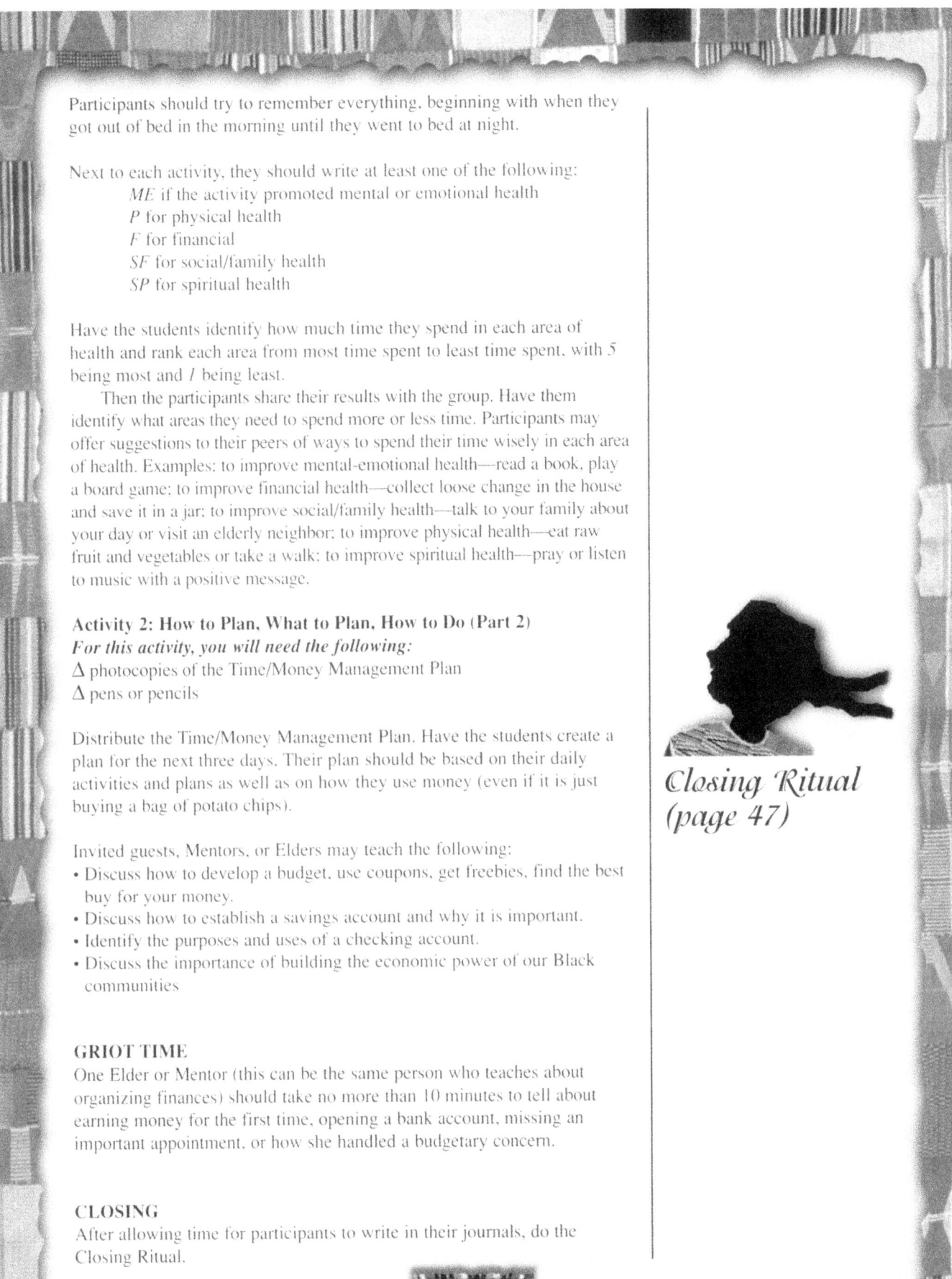

Closing Ritual (page 47)

Time/Money Management Plan

Plan three days by writing the activity in the time slot of the area(s) of health the activity will affect. If money is involved, write in the amount.

Date _____ Time	Physical Health	Mental-Emotional Health	Family/Social Health	Spiritual health
7–8 a.m.				
8–9 a.m.				
9–10 a.m.				
10–11 a.m.				
11am–12pm				
12–1 p.m.				
1–2 p.m.				
2–3 p.m.				
3–4 p.m.				
4–5 p.m.				
5–6 p.m.				
6–7 p.m.				
7–8 p.m.				
8–9 p.m.				
9–10 p.m.				
10–11 p.m.				

Date _____ Time	Physical Health	Mental-Emotional Health	Family/Social Health	Spiritual health
7–8 a.m.				
8–9 a.m.				
9–10 a.m.				
10–11 a.m.				
11am–12pm				
12–1 p.m.				
1–2 p.m.				
2–3 p.m.				
3–4 p.m.				
4–5 p.m.				
5–6 p.m.				
6–7 p.m.				
7–8 p.m.				
8–9 p.m.				
9–10 p.m.				
10–11 p.m.				

Date _____ Time	Physical Health	Mental-Emotional Health	Family/Social Health	Spiritual health
7–8 a.m.				
8–9 a.m.				
9–10 a.m.				
10–11 a.m.				
11am–12pm				
12–1 p.m.				
1–2 p.m.				
2–3 p.m.				
3–4 p.m.				
4–5 p.m.				
5–6 p.m.				
6–7 p.m.				
7–8 p.m.				
8–9 p.m.				
9–10 p.m.				
10–11 p.m.				

Permission is granted to the purchaser to photocopy this page for use with DAUGHTERS OF IMANI: A CHRISTIAN RITES OF PASSAGE FOR AFRICAN-AMERICAN YOUNG WOMEN, © 2005 by Abingdon Press. All rights reserved.

Organize Your Time

Organize and set priorities for your schedule. Effective and efficient people keep a notebook and a calendar of events. On the page below, list all of the tasks or activities you want to do today. Then assign an A next to all of the tasks or activities that are the most important. You may write an A next to more than one thing. After you prioritize all of the As, do B next, and C next to the least important.

Write the 10 things you would like to accomplish today.
Assign an "A, B, C" to each. Check off when finished.

Things I Want to Accomplish Today

Priority
(A, B, C)   **Finished**

_____ 1. _____ ☐

_____ 2. _____ ☐

_____ 3. _____ ☐

_____ 4. _____ ☐

_____ 5. _____ ☐

_____ 6. _____ ☐

_____ 7. _____ ☐

_____ 8. _____ ☐

_____ 9. _____ ☐

_____ 10. _____ ☐

Permission is granted to the purchaser to photocopy this page for use with **DAUGHTERS OF IMANI: A CHRISTIAN RITES OF PASSAGE FOR AFRICAN-AMERICAN YOUNG WOMEN**, © 2005 by Abingdon Press. All rights reserved.

Emerging Womanhood Graduate Exam

This comprehensive open-book exam should be distributed to initiates who are preparing to cross over to the threshold of young adulthood. Initiates have one month to complete the exam. The Ohemma and Council of Elders should read over the exams and offer feedback and comments to the initiates in an informal setting outside of the normal meeting time.

Answer the following questions on a separate sheet of paper:

1. Who is God, Jesus, and the Holy Spirit, according to the Bible and your own experience?

2. If you were to honor a historical African American with a national holiday, who would it be? Why?

3. List 8 values or character traits that are important to you, and explain their significance in your life.

4. What is the difference between a checking account and a savings account? What are some methods that people use to invest their money?

5. Choose a woman who you believe demonstrates the gift of leadership. Write a short essay about her. Include the leadership qualities they possess. What makes her a leader, how is she making a difference in the world?

6. What does *STD* stand for? Name 5 STDs and tell how they are contracted. What are the symptoms for males and females, and what is the cure for each disease you named?

7. Have the arts always been important in the culture of African people? If so, how?

8. What is the benefit of using daily, monthly, weekly calendars? What is the benefit of organization in one's life?

9. Read 1 Corinthians 13, write a summary of the passage, and discuss why this passage is important for all Christians.

10. Please write your short-term goals for the next year, your medium range goals for the next 3–5 years, and your long-range goals for the next 10 years.

11. Name the organs that make up the male and female reproductive system. Using the language of human sexuality, explain how a woman becomes pregnant. What is the context for sexual relationships, according to the Bible?

12. Define *nervous breakdown*. What contributes to a nervous breakdown? How does one avoid having a nervous breakdown?

13. Define *friendship*. Write a newspaper want ad that describes what you look for in a true friendship.

Suggested Resources
(In Order of Appearance)

Chapter 4: Mentor Training
1. *Showing Mary: How Women Can Share Prayers, Wisdom, and the Blessings of God*, by Renita Weems (Walk Worthy Books, 2002; ISBN: 0446530662)

Chapter 5: Membership
2. *Extreme Faith Youth Bible: Contemporary English Version* (American Bible Society, 2000; ISBN: 1585160660)
3. *The Real Deal: A Spiritual Guide for Black Teen Girls*, by Billie Montgomery Cook (Judson Press, 2004; ISBN: 0817014586)
4. *Prayers That Avail Much for Teens*, by Germaine Copeland (Harrison House, 2002; ISBN: 1577946006)

Chapter 7: Rituals
5. *Racism 101*, by Nikki Giovanni (William Morrow and Co., 1995; ISBN: 0688142346)

Unit 1: Self-Esteem
6. *No Disrespect*, by Sister Souljah (Vintage Books, 1996; ISBN: 0679767088)
7. *Out of Eden—This Is Your Life* (DVD) (Emi Distribution, 2002)
8. *Wouldn't Take Nothing for My Journey Now*, by Maya Angelou (Bantam Books, 1997; ISBN: 0769427430)
9. *Maya Angelou: Poems*, by Maya Angelou (Bantam Books, 1986; ISBN: 0553255762)
10. *Still I Rise*, by Maya Angelou (Bantam Books, 1980; ISBN: 0553131362)
11. *Make a Joyful Sound: Poems for Children by African-American Poets*, edited by Deborah Slier (Scholastic Books, 1996; ISBN: 0590674323)
12. *Racism 101*, by Nikki Giovanni (William Morrow and Co., 1995; ISBN: 0688142346)
13. *Narrative of Sojourner Truth*, by Sojourner Truth (Dover Publications, 1997; ISBN: 048629899X)
14. *Crossing the Danger Water: Three Hundred Years of African-American Writing*, edited by Deirdre Mullane (Anchor Books, 1993; ISBN: 0385422431)
15. *Epic Lives: One Hundred Black Women Who Made a Difference*, edited by Jessie Carney Smith (Visible Ink Press, 1993; ISBN: 081039426X)
16. *Discover Your God-Given Gifts*, by Don and Katie Fortune (Chosen Books Publishers, 1987; ISBN: 0800791088)

Unit 2: Endurance and Bonding/Family Matters
17. *Guide My Feet: Prayers and Meditations for Our Children*, Marian Wright Edelman (HarperPerennial, 2000; ISBN: 00609588197)
18. "Last Will and Testament," by Mary McLeod Bethune

Unit 3: Health and Sexuality
19. *The Black Women's Health Book: Speaking for Ourselves*, edited by Evelyn C. White (Publishers Group West, 1994; ISBN: 1878067400)
20. *What Your Mother Never Told You About S-e-x*, Hilda Hutcherson, M.D. (Perigee, 2002; ISBN: 0399528539)
21. *Brown Sugar* (DVD) (Twentieth Century Fox, 2002) (Preview the movie before showing it to your group.)

Unit 4: Social Grace
22. *Soul Food* (rated R) (DVD) (Twentieth Century Fox, 1997) (Preview the movie before showing it to your group.)

Additional Resources
- *African-American Heritage Teaching Cards* (package of 20) (Abingdon Press, 2001; ISBN: 0687049997)

- *African-American Heritage Posters* (Abingdon Press, 2001; ISBN: 0687050294)

- CDs of spiritual, classical, and jazz music

Bibliography

Bates, Karen Grigsby; and Hudson, Karen, *Basic Black: Home Training for Modern Times* (Broadway, 2002).

Dial, Steven N., Sr., *The Lessons of Life to Achieve Your Dreams* (Orman Press, 2001).

Ferebee, Janice, et al, *Got It Goin' On II: Power Tools for Girls* (Ferebee Enterprises Intl., 2000).

Freeman, Darrell V., *Investing in Our African-American Youth—Can You Handle It?* (Truth Bible Institute, 1994).

Kunjufu, Jawanza. *Hip-Hop vs. MAAT—A Psycho/Social Analysis of Values* (African American Images, 1993).

Lewis, Barbara A., *What Do You Stand for?—A Kid's Guide to Understanding Character* (Free Spirit Publishing, 1997).

Lewis, Mary C., *Herstory: Black Female Rites of Passage* (African American Images, 1988).

McNair, Chris, *Young Lions: Christian Rites of Passage for African-American Young Men* (Abingdon Press, 2001)

Moore, Mafori, *Transformation: A Rites of Passage Manual for African American Girls* (Stars Press, 1987).

Thompson, Bernida, *Black Madonnas and Young Lions—A Rites of Passage for U.S. African Adolescents* (Roots Activity Learning Center, 1992).

Willis, Bruce. *The Adinkra Dictionary: A Visual Primer in the Language of Adinkra* (Pyramid Complex, 1998; out of print).

Wright, Madeline. *Sisters Helping Sisters: The Wheeler Avenue Baptist Church Girls' Rites of Passage Program* (African American Images, 1997).

www.ingramcontent.com/pod-product-compliance
Lightning Source LLC
Chambersburg PA
CBHW081544090426
42743CB00014BA/3130